Psychological Therapies with Older People

Sigmund Freud believed that psychoanalysis (and other forms of therapy) was not suitable for people over 50 years of age. In *Psychological Therapies with Older People*, the authors demonstrate the value of a range of psychological interventions with older people, showing that it is 'not too late' to help.

With an emphasis on practical application and using a wide range of clinical examples, the authors describe the therapies most likely to be useful in a mental health service for older people, and consider the implications for service provision. Therapies covered include:

- Interpersonal therapy (IPT)
- Cognitive behaviour therapy (CBT)
- Psychodynamic and systemic therapy
- Cognitive analytical therapy (CAT)

For each treatment, the historical background and basic theoretical model is summarised before giving a description of the therapy in practice. The authors also discuss the theory of the use of evidence of efficacy and effectiveness in choosing therapeutic interventions, summarising currently available data. *Psychological Therapies with Older People* will be an invaluable resource for psychiatrists and psychologists working with older people, as well as for GPs, nurses and occupational therapists.

Jason Hepple is a Consultant Psychiatrist, a Cognitive Analytic Therapy Practitioner and an Honorary Fellow of Exeter University.

Jane Pearce is a Consultant Psychiatrist in the Department of Psychiatry of Old Age in Oxfordshire Mental Healthcare NHS Trust.

Philip Wilkinson is a Consultant Psychiatrist in the Department of Psychiatry of Old Age in Oxfordshire Mental Healthcare NHS Trust and a Cognitive Behaviour Therapist.

Psychological Therapies with Older People

Developing treatments for effective practice

Edited by Jason Hepple, Jane Pearce and Philip Wilkinson

BRUNNER-ROUTLEDGE
ALERE FLAMMAM
Taylor & Francis Group

First published 2002 by Brunner-Routledge
27 Church Road, Hove, East Sussex BN3 2FA

Simultaneously published in the USA and Canada
by Taylor & Francis Inc
29 West 35th Street, New York, NY 10001

Brunner-Routledge is an imprint of the Taylor & Francis Group

© 2002 Selection and editorial matter, Jason Hepple, Jane Pearce and
Philip Wilkinson. Individual chapters, the contributors.

Typeset in Sabon by RefineCatch Limited, Bungay, Suffolk
Printed and bound in Great Britain by TJ International,
Padstow, Cornwall

Cover design by Louise Page

British Library Cataloguing in Publication Data
A catalogue record for this book is available from the British Library

ISBN 1–58391–136–7 (hbk)
ISBN 1–58391–137–5 (pbk)

Contents

List of figures and boxes

Figures

Boxes

Notes on contributors

Mark Ardern has worked as a Consultant in Old Age Psychiatry at St Charles Hospital, West London, since 1984. He is a founder member and currently Chairman of the Older Adults Section of the Association for Psychoanalytic Psychotherapy in the National Health Service.

Jason Hepple is a Consultant Psychiatrist, a Cognitive Analytic Therapy Practitioner and an Honorary Fellow of Exeter University, UK. He works predominantly with older people in Somerset and the South West of England and has researched the outcomes of attempted suicide in this group. He is developing psychotherapeutic models to help in the management of personality disorder and pseudo-dementia in later life and is a champion for older persons' services and the more widespread availability of psychological therapies.

Mike Hobbs is a Consultant Psychiatrist in Psychotherapy and Clinical Director with the Oxfordshire Mental Healthcare NHS Trust, and Honorary Senior Clinical Lecturer at the University of Oxford, UK. He has trained in psychodynamic psychotherapy, group analysis and cognitive therapy. His academic interests include the psychiatric effects of complex trauma, and the treatment of severe personality disorder.

Mark Miller is Associate Professor of Psychiatry at the Western Psychiatric Institute and Clinic at the University of Pittsburgh Medical Center, and serves as Medical Director of the Center of Evaluation and Treatment of Late-life Depression in Pittsburgh, USA. He is actively involved in teaching at the university. His research interests are geriatric psychiatry, bereavement, and medical co-morbidity in late-life depression.

Jane Pearce works as a Consultant Old Age Psychiatrist in Oxford, UK. She was introduced to family therapy in the Department of Psychotherapy at the Warneford Hospital, Oxford, and has experience in setting up and working in family therapy within old age psychiatric services. She has published on the management of atypical chest pain, functional somatic symptoms in the elderly and psychological symptoms in the menopause.

Charles F. Reynolds III is Professor of Psychiatry, Neurology and Neuroscience and Director of Mental Health Intervention at the Research Center for the Study of Late-life Mood Disorders at the University of Pittsburgh Medical Center, USA. His primary research interests are mood and sleep disorders of later life with a particular focus on treatment, mechanisms of treatment response and suicide prevention.

Laura Sutton is a Consultant Clinical Psychologist currently working in Suffolk, UK. She has been a major influence on the development and application of Cognitive Analytic Therapy in working with older people.

Philip Wilkinson is a Consultant in the Psychiatry of Old Age in Oxford, UK, where he trained in cognitive therapy. He is involved in the promotion of psychological treatments in the care of older patients, and teaches on the use of cognitive therapy. He has published on problem-solving psychotherapy and liaison psychiatry services and his current research interests include the evaluation of cognitive behaviour therapy with older adults.

Foreword

Mike Hobbs

In contrast with the long-held and prejudicial view that older people do not have the mental flexibility to benefit from psychotherapy, increasing numbers of clinicians now recognise the value of offering psychological treatments to their older patients. Indeed, in the UK and elsewhere, national strategies state clearly that psychological therapies are integral to comprehensive mental health provision for older people, and our elders will come to expect the same access to psychological therapies as adults of working age. In response, this ground-breaking book offers the clinician an invaluable guide to an important and broad range of contemporary therapies.

The range of the psychotherapy models practised with older adults owes much to history and the creative energies of their originators and practitioners. This is recognised by the authors of this book who begin each chapter with a brief account of the background to each therapy. Some psychological therapies have long been practised with elders while others have been introduced more recently. Some are better known than others in certain parts of the world. Each model, however, has its own more or less comprehensive theoretical underpinning and rationale for clinical practice. These too are laid out clearly in each chapter.

One advantage of the limited attention given over the years to psychological therapies for older people is that there are fewer traditions, preconceptions and vested interests to constrain the development of ideas and practice. This should make it easier both to apply established models and to introduce new models of therapy to meet the specific needs of older people. One important process has been the modification of longer-established treatment models to meet the expectations of both the users and the commissioners of mental health services. For example, modifications to classical psychoanalytic technique have led to the progressive development and research evaluation of short-term models of psychodynamic therapy which are effective, applicable and highly acceptable to older people. Their emphasis on an active, focal and time-limited approach, with integral attention to the dynamics of ending, separation and loss is very relevant to the older population. The opportunities presented by the development of psychological therapies for older people have also encouraged the application of newer models of therapy, some of which represent judicious integrations of theory and practice derived from more established models. The potential for such exciting innovation comes over in this book. Cognitive analytic therapy is one exciting approach which is proving highly acceptable to patients with a range of mental health problems, including personality disorder. Interpersonal psychotherapy has a compelling theoretical, clinical and scientific base. It is also a short-term model which is quickly learned by therapists, offering the attraction of ready application in hard-pressed mental health services for the elderly.

In Chapters 2 to 6, the editors and invited authors employ a common format for their accounts of the models of therapy that are offered most frequently by mental health services for older people: psychodynamic therapy (Mark Ardern), cognitive behaviour therapy (Philip Wilkinson), systemic therapy (Jane Pearce), interpersonal psychotherapy (Mark Miller and Charles F. Reynolds III) and cognitive analytic therapy (Jason Hepple). Each adopts a practical approach to descriptions of the therapy model and the selection of patients. Clinical illustrations bring to life their accounts of how the therapy is practised. Sufficient emphasis is given to technical considerations to allow the reader an informed view of what each treatment model involves for both patient and therapist, and how therapeutic interventions are tailored to the needs of each individual patient. These therapies have several qualities in common. They are usually short-term, focused and goal- or solution-directed, and involve an active and collaborative working relationship between patient and therapist. Each may be used as a discrete and specific treatment, as a component of a broader treatment programme, or as a conceptual framework underpinning a broader management plan.

Efforts have been made to identify more systematically the models of psychotherapy that are most efficacious in the treatment of specific mental health problems. Roth and Fonagy's influential text *What Works for Whom? A Critical Review of Psychotherapy Research* (Woods and Roth 1996) includes a short chapter addressing the psychological problems of late life in general, and those associated with organic disorders more specifically. The authors acknowledge that older people are less likely to receive psychological treatments and that there has been little research into their efficacy with this age group. They go on to identify data confirming the effectiveness of therapies and cite evidence to suggest that group therapies may be helpful in preventing relapse. The volume of scientific evidence for the effectiveness of different therapy models varies widely and, with the exception of interpersonal therapy, much of the high-quality research so far has been undertaken with adults of working age. This is not to say that other established therapies should be abandoned but that all therapies should be practised competently, evaluated systematically and the development of sound scientific evidence should be a priority. There is much that remains to be done.

The contribution of psychological methods of treatment to mental health provision for older people is now beginning to be addressed in strategic policy. Of course, the task of moving beyond political rhetoric to the realisation of this ambitious goal is enormous. The continuing commitment of policy makers, health service commissioners, and service providers will be crucial. From ground level, however, the views of older people themselves and the vision, pressure and achievements of clinicians who work with them will prove essential for success. Where there is a will, there is a way! The older people who use mental health services, and their carers, will need to expect and ask for psychological therapies both as adjuncts and as alternatives to physical methods of treatment. Clinicians of all relevant professions will need to feel empowered to develop and provide effective psychotherapies for their older patients. Very little that would assist them has yet been published, either in the form of clinical material or scientific research. This book offers welcome support by providing the relevant information required for realistic development of the aims and competences upon which this achievement will be based.

In this book, the authors achieve their goal of giving a consistent, systematic and practical account of a range of therapies. In their concluding chapter, Jason Hepple, Jane Pearce and Philip Wilkinson go on to explore how the psychotherapies described can be integrated into clinical practice within mental health services for elders.

Further attention is given to examination of the factors that are specific to the psychological treatment of older patients, with reference also to the settings and institutions in which these are practised. An overview is given of an evidence-based approach to therapies. A book that is aimed at helping older patients would not be complete, however, without a view of the developmental challenges of ageing and patients' perspectives on therapy. This is provided in an introductory chapter by Laura Sutton which, compared with the practical emphasis of the book as a whole, offers wider theoretical and personal perspectives.

The editors have successfully achieved their aim of producing a highly readable book which will be of interest to all those who work with older adults in mental health services and in other agencies, regardless of profession; and it will also prove to be of interest to psychotherapists and counsellors who are not accustomed to working with elders. It may well encourage some to extend their expertise by developing the skills necessary for psychotherapeutic work with older patients. Because this book does not assume specialist knowledge of medicine or psychology, it may also be of interest to those (including families) who care for older people, and indeed to the older people themselves to whom these psychotherapies are dedicated. This would be a fitting tribute to those who conceived and wrote it.

Reference

Woods, R. and Roth, A. (1996) 'Effectiveness of psychological interventions with older people', in A. Roth and P. Fonagy (eds) *What works for whom? A critical review of psychotherapy research*. New York: Guilford Press.

Preface

As clinicians we have, for a number of years, been applying psychological treatment skills in our general mental health services for older people. We have often been restrained, however, from developing formal psychological treatment services when encouragement, support and supervision have been lacking. Consequently, despite the increasing pool of evidence to support their effectiveness, psychological interventions are not widely available to older people here in the United Kingdom. There appears to be a number of reasons for this. First, we believe that a lack of guidance on the application of psychological theory and practice plays an important role. How are the therapies actually practised with older people? What are the situations in which a given therapy might be helpful? How are people selected? What are the main activities of the therapy? How well does a therapy fit with other treatments or co-existing conditions? Secondly, later-life problems are frequently viewed from a biological rather than a psychological perspective and resources are allocated on that basis. Priority is therefore given to physical and social treatment methods.

In this text we have, together with Mike Hobbs, looked at the psychological therapies broadly available for patients of all ages and identified those most likely to be useful and practical in a mental health service for older people. For the purposes of this book, we have not included core psychosocial interventions for dementia such as validation, dementia care mapping and the expressive therapies.

We hope that this book will create momentum for the application of psychological therapies with older people. It is intended for professionals who have direct contact with older people facing personal difficulties, losses, illnesses or age-related changes in their lives. The emphasis is on application. We hope that this very practical approach will stimulate interest in referring patients for therapy as well as encouraging practitioners to acquire training themselves. As this book requires little specialist knowledge, we hope it may also be helpful to potential patients and those who care for and about them.

We have been supported by a number of our colleagues. Mike Hobbs has been especially encouraging and helpful to us in this venture. We are also immensely grateful to the other authors who have contributed so willingly to this text. Martha Lewis has captured the individual and personal context for us in her artwork at the beginning of the book. We have been privileged to have worked with many people as patients. We would like to particularly thank those who have been willing for us to describe some of their experiences in therapy so that others may learn or benefit. All case material has been made anonymous or names have been changed. Elsewhere when we refer to individual patients we have usually adopted a convention of calling them 'her' simply because there are more older women.

Jane Pearce and Philip Wilkinson, Oxford
Jason Hepple, Yeovil
July 2001

Acknowledgements

We are enormously grateful to a number of colleagues who share our enthusiasm for psychological treatments and have helped us to discover what is possible with older adults. In particular we extend our thanks to Sydney Bloch, Melanie Fennell, Dolores Gallagher-Thompson, Matthew Ganda, Sue Kühn, Norma Maple, Helen Matthews, Harriet Montgomery, Anthony Ryle, Eva Smith and Larry Thompson.

Our interest also owes much to those who have worked hard to promote good old age psychiatry services and training in Oxford, in particular Steve Corea, Robin Jacoby, Catherine Oppenheimer and John Robinson.

On a personal level, we would like to thank Mark Dawson, Anthony Heath, Denise and George Hepple, and Christine Warriner for their support and encouragement.

Thanks are also due to Janet George for her considerable secretarial help.

Most importantly, we wish to thank our patients who have shared their experiences with us.

Chapter 1

Introduction

Contemporary views – a duel with the past

Laura Sutton

Few people in the UK receive personal therapy in old age. A recent survey of 100 departments of psychotherapy in the UK concluded that compared with younger people the provision of services to older and elderly people is woefully lacking, with only a tiny number receiving therapy (Murphy 2000). In this chapter I examine the novelty of therapy in old age. First, in the account of her therapy by a client as she is forced to encounter her life's ending, expressing her experience of her therapy and what she gained from it, I aim to show how her therapy was shaped by a variety of tensions in the development of psychological therapies and psychotherapies, particularly in relation to how they position themselves with respect to 'present' and 'past'. Implications for this when working with older people in therapy will be explored, particularly in relation to issues of authenticity and the '(re)historying of the self' in society.

The novelty of therapy in old age

Britton and Woods (1999) note the roots of modern-day psychology in psychometric testing and say that we need to move on from this. They explain that one of the central ethical issues surrounding working with older and elderly people now is that of power. In the realm of psychometric testing, they note that 'psychometric tests may similarly be the means of power: they may be used to give a diagnosis that is used to "explain" actions and behaviours that will then never be understood' (p. 17). They go on to chart the progress of the therapies in psychology for older people, with the emergence of behavioural and cognitive therapies, the newer interest in psychodynamic and systemic approaches, as well as those therapies seen more as the province of old age such as reminiscence and

Reality Orientation. They also highlight that in all this there has not been concomitant adequate theoretical development, especially in developmental theory:

> The absence of the lifespan developmental perspective from mainstream psychology should be acknowledged . . . what is required is not simply more studies specifically on older people, or comparisons of older and younger people on yet more aspects of cognition, but rather studies that reflect the psychological functioning of people across the lifespan, and which seek to make sense of individual differences.
>
> (Britton and Woods 1999, pp. 10, 11)

This is interesting because they suggest that we need to move on from psychometric testing, only for its attendant language – that of individual differences – to be let back in by the back door. Pilgrim and Treacher (1992) explain that in order to distinguish itself from medicine/psychoanalysis, psychology as a burgeoning discipline aligned itself with emergent notions of science so that 'The dominant tradition associated with British psychology in its first official fifty years was to be that of studying individual differences' (Pilgrim and Treacher 1992, p. 24).

Similarly in psychotherapy, Knight (1996, 1999) rejects what he terms the 'loss deficit paradigm' which he says is part of the practitioner heritage in psychotherapy, in which old age is characterised as a series of losses, with depression the typical response. He is rather in favour of integrating psychotherapy and scientific gerontology. For instance, he extends Piaget's model of intellectual development, drawing on studies that attest to the developing emotional and cognitive complexity with age. Knight argues on these bases that old age is a time of 'post-formal' reasoning characterised by a dialectical understanding, that is, by a greater understanding of the nature of social change and a greater appreciation that people hold different points of view. Studies have shown that older people are generally less driven by anxiety than younger people, and are less impulsive, so have a greater capacity for tolerating ambiguities and openness (Knight 1996, 1999).

Knight reaches a position similar to that of Britton and Woods (1999), namely that a contextual, cohort and maturity-based model for ageing is needed. He, Britton and Woods (1999) and Coleman (1999) all cite Erikson's work (Erikson 1950, Erikson *et al.* 1986) as notable amongst the few to attempt a lifespan model of development. Knight explains that Erikson reinterpreted childhood development in less sexual terms than classical analysis, and extended personality development into adolescence and adulthood, and old age. Yet Knight says,

> Social change which occurs before or during our childhood years may be taken for granted; that which occurs during our adult years will be truly experienced as change. These differences, while not developmental, are real.
>
> Much of change in adulthood and old age is not so much an ontogenetic unfolding of personality development as it is the assumption and discarding of social roles which are roughly age linked, although less so in the 1990s than in earlier decades.
>
> (Knight 1996, pp. 298 and 301)

Knight is placing development as outside real social change, and ontogeny as something which happens before ageing does. Thus, while Knight is advocating a contemporary integrating of psychotherapy and scientific gerontology to develop a maturity-based model of development over a lifetime, his words also replay a traditional view of ontological development, as though the formative years of personality development are those only of childhood.

In both texts it is as if we are seeing the voices of our forebears alongside our own, despite attempts to disassociate from them. This parallels some of the struggles in therapy with those in old age, in intergenerational issues of continuity and discontinuity, of association and dissociation or integration and disintegration (Erikson *et al.* 1986).

I would like to draw this out further, beginning with Lilian's therapy.

Lilian

Lilian was in her early seventies when she was referred to her local Community Mental Health Team because of compulsive hand and face washing. She had had periods of compulsive hand and face washing since her adolescence which she had been able to cope with independently up until now, but she was feeling increasingly out of control following a diagnosis of malignant facial cancer. She had increased her rituals to forty times per day which was making her depressed and afraid to socialise. Her Community Mental Health Nurse, Moira, came to me for supervision.

Lilian had sixteen sessions with Moira, with a three-month follow-up. We drew on Salkovskis and Kirk (1989) to orientate Moira to a cognitive-behavioural approach to obsessive compulsive disorders, meantime holding the process issues (Lilian's – and Moira's – need for emotional containment) within supervision, especially given Lilian's fear for her life now. This is Lilian's account of her therapy.

> For a long time I have felt unable to write this account of my illness and treatment. I believe this is because I could not bear to see the facts in cold print, although these facts are always present in my mind and cannot be dismissed in the foreseeable future.
>
> In July 1999, following analysis of tissues taken from my face after surgery, I was found to have a serious skin cancer which is invasive and as threatening as melanoma in possible consequences. It is very aggressive and any lesion above 2 cm in length has a life expectancy for the patient of five years. Therefore I am examined by a specialist every three months for signs of a return.
>
> At first, after receiving the diagnosis, I was numb. After I had absorbed the information I felt paralysed with fear, unable to concentrate, to sleep or eat properly and was very restless by day and night. I was prescribed Prozac daily, Valium to be taken when very shaky with sleeping tablets to be used sparingly. As the Prozac began to act I found I could eat and sleep better and I tried to wean myself off Valium. I succeeded reasonably well in this but then began to have physical symptoms in the form of a neck rash, acute acid indigestion, sore throats and a compulsion to wash my hands repeatedly resulting in damaged sore skin on my hands.
>
> I had tried private stress therapy which had limited effect. Then was given counselling at the hospice but the symptoms continued. Every small spot sent me into panic and I became a too frequent visitor to the doctor's surgery. After some weeks of this I was referred to the community mental health team and Moira came to my home to treat me.
>
> I was not hopeful at first about improving my depressed state, but in response to her firm but sympathetic attitude I

began to open out to my innermost fears and to face the situation more calmly and without feeling I was being selfish as I did when trying to talk to my husband when I knew I was distressing him. Without this chance to speak openly about my guilt feelings and terror of the future I believe I would have collapsed with full breakdown.

First, I had to learn that I could not escape my problems. *Acknowledgement*. Second, to realise that should the cancer return I would not be shunned like a leper by those I loved. I was not unclean as I had thought, but unfortunate like many millions of others with the disease throughout the world. In short *Acceptance*. A long lesson this and it was tough to grapple with those destructive thoughts that crept like rats through any quiet moment to start their ceaseless scratching. I was asked to keep a written record of my stress levels in various situations, for example when resisting an impulse to wash my hands as a response to inner turmoil. Throughout this long phase I also unearthed and revealed to Moira earlier distressing life events which had affected me, I now knew, at a subconscious level. I was aware that absolute honesty was vital despite the pain of re-living things I had felt were well buried. From Moira, I understood that cognitive-behavioural therapy was a method of making me aware of how undisciplined destructive thought will weaken reasoning ability and result in obsessive attitudes and actions. These in turn nurture panic attacks and physical symptoms arising from strain.

The final step was *Adjustment*. A difficult but rewarding period. I learned by painful repetition to control panic attacks by breathing techniques and a gradually forming ability to talk myself calm whatever my fears. Not the least of the benefits was a new evaluation of myself and a belief that I can and will cope should the cancer return, now that I realise that I am not unclean and do not deserve to suffer.

The whole process took from February to July. I was glad to receive this treatment in my own home as it made me feel less of a 'case'. I remain as co-ordinator of a riding school, a volunteer at a training bureau, and go to an art class. My Christian faith has helped me in ways impossible to quantify and remains a strong factor in recovery of my spiritual health.

In relation to Lilian's words about her illness and treatment, it was clearly important to her that she felt less of a 'case'. It is as if she is speaking out against the internalisation of a powerful medical discourse framing distress, in part a depersonalising discourse. To pathologise her further, we believe, would have replayed the dissociations she had lived out of so far. As her story unfolded it became clearer how she had become the way she had within the dynamics of her family, society and the culture surrounding her over time, present and past.

What to do with all that

Lilian was in shock, with her fear and panic, and despair in the face of the threat to her life, all the while carrying a fear of full breakdown. Moira was an experienced practitioner close in age to Lilian – both, as Moira put it, with a 'degree from the university of life'. Yet she was daunted by the prospect of conducting Lilian's therapy. She couldn't see how she was going to keep to the CBT model to help Lilian with her obsessional rituals while she was so distraught about her cancer. Reading the CBT text didn't help Moira with this. It spoke largely of cognitions and behaviours, with techniques for accessing cognitions and devising behavioural experiments to challenge such cognitions. It is a peculiarly abstracted language which gives little or no sense of what people's struggles are over their lives.

This predicament reminds me of debates within the cognitive psychology of memory between the 'purists' and 'ecologists' of memory (Sutton 1995). In the early 1900s with experimental psychology came the experimental approach to memory. This is predicated on the 'mind body' split of classic Cartesian dualism (Still and Costall 1991). 'Memory' is taken as one of the cognitive faculties – in other words, a faculty of the mind. Experiments are then designed to try and measure aspects of *pure* memory (rather than 'remembering' which they regard as affected by all sorts of extraneous factors, such as 'emotion' – that is, 'body'). Ebbinghaus's early experiments on the recall of nonsense syllables are often used as a historical marker of the beginnings of the experimental approach to memory.

By the 1970s frustration had grown. In 1978 Ulric Neisser addressed the first conference on the practical aspects of memory in Cardiff, UK (Gruneberg and Morris 1992). He said that whilst we know a lot about remembering nonsense syllables, lists of words and so on in the context of the laboratory, we have ended up not knowing very much about remembering other things in everyday contexts (Neisser 1978). Neisser's address, in turn, is taken as one of the historical markers of the developing interest in the practical aspects of memory.

I suspect that similar philosophical problems were at work in Moira's dilemma, in that the abstract language of cognitions and behaviours made it hard for her to connect to real things. Moira was encouraged, though, by Lilian's bringing a CBT book with her to her first session. She told me that Lilian had sat a long way away from her. I felt that there was more happening here than conventional CBT could accommodate. In its break with medicine, psychoanalysis and philosophy (particularly hermeneutics, which is the study of meaning, see Freeman 1993), psychology detached itself from transference and countertransference – 'feelings' – in favour of the new objectivity, of rationality and measurement, with the root metaphor of 'man as scientist' and the root behaviour as experimentation. One effect of this was to give us the behavioural and cognitive therapies, leading the way I suspect for the development of other brief focal therapies and leading the challenge to produce evidence for the effectiveness of any therapy.

Beck (1989) explains that the cognitive therapy he sought to develop at the time was a way of responding to the neglect of the *conscious* mind in analytic and behavioural therapies alike. The former sought to discover unconscious processes to which the analyst but not the analysand was privy. The latter ignored subjectivity on the grounds that it was not observable directly. Beck (1989) argued that in so doing neither allows for the reasoning abilities and thoughtfulness of the client equally as much as those of the therapist, hence the collaborative project of cognitive therapy. I also wonder if this was in part an embodiment of social changes post-war in the way that people related to each other, with a less formal and more technological society.

At the same time, the scientific metaphor in its language of rational objectivity inevitably put a distance between therapist and client. It is as if, like a scientist, the therapist is 'discovering' the cognitions and schemata of the other. So although the collaborative project was set and developed, the scientific metaphor may also limit it (Ryle 1997). It embodies a markedly different frame of reference from that of two people in relation as people, which is perhaps more linked to the hermeneutic frame (Freeman 1993). Coleman (1996), for instance, remarks that 'Dementia care reveals clearly how our personhood depends ultimately upon each other.' I think that these philosophical differences, as well as psychology's break from philosophy through which such differences could be named and thought about, have made it difficult for cognitive psychologies to re-integrate transference and countertransference as they are trying to do (e.g. Dick *et al.* 1999).

Ryle (1997) has addressed some of these problems, as part of what he has called the need for a common language for the therapies; perhaps, current moves towards integrative therapies are the response to the disintegration so far. With its influences from personal construct therapy, self-psychology and its restatement of classical object relations theory of psychoanalysis, as well as CBT precise descriptions of patterns, CAT now attends to relational processes that influence how we become 'in ourselves'. A core idea is that of reciprocal roles (e.g. Ryle 1994). Whereas CBT, for instance, is oriented to the detail of cognitions and behaviours as part of its foundations in objectivity, CAT is orientated to self-processes within repertoires of reciprocal roles, and as such is one of the new 'dialogic' approaches to therapy (Margison 2000). This is part of the contemporary 'turn to the text', found elsewhere in discourse analysis and the like (Burman and Parker 1993). A 'text' can be as much a bodily 'text' as verbal and so is released from classic Cartesian dualism.

In this regard I wondered how Lilian had come to live her life. I wondered whether she had coped practically on her own (she had coped independently with her hand washing till now), somehow not able to get close to people (her distance from Moira). I wondered about possible disconnections in Lilian's life. My concern was that she and Moira could unwittingly replay a collusive positive transference in which they worked quickly on behavioural goals via the technology of CBT, but did not integrate her distress. In other words, the lack of care in technically good cognitive-behavioural therapy could repeat past experiences of lack of care.

Predictably, Lilian produced technically good diaries (which is unusual). She also said quietly to Moira that it was hard. This was the same distant part of her that sat removed from Moira in quiet despair. Lilian could easily have become dispirited, that is, performing well (in therapy) but soldiering on – rather a pattern in her life (Ryle 1997). I encouraged Moira to keep this in mind, so that rather than being distracted by Lilian's competency (as if that meant it was going well), she continued to let Lilian have lots of space to 'debrief' on life at the same time as not losing focus on her 'exposure' and the 'response prevention' of classic CBT. She needed to trust that Lilian could work actively on her goals (after all, that was her strength) as she was guided more in how to share, as this was what she wasn't used to. This experience of care, holding her capacities and incapacities, was being formed in the human and therapeutic relationship that Moira had with Lilian. Lilian wasn't a 'case of OCD (Obsessive–Compulsive Disorder) plus cancer'. Rather, I wanted her clear potential for personal integration to be realised, for her future, present and past, as part of her family.

Lilian came to share with Moira experiences in her family life which she and her family had 'washed their hands of' long ago. Courageously, Lilian broached these things with her family. She found that they were courageous too and able to talk. By the end of her therapy there was a sense of some restitution. Lilian was free of obsessive hand and face washing and was sitting close to Moira and had resumed her socialising, which was still the case at follow-up.

What is to become of me?

CBT presents itself as concerned mostly with the 'here and now'; traditional analytic therapy inclined to the effects of early dynamics. Yet, how Lilian was in the 'here and now' was in a sense how she had always been through her life, even as a child : the self-sufficient coper unable to connect and share with others what she and others had carried on their own. Arguably there was a transformative aspect here, where the benefits of her therapy to Lilian were not least of all her reaching a new evaluation of herself: as someone who is not unclean and does not deserve to suffer.

Whereas in mainstream cognitive psychology the emphasis is on what one has become – as in the testing of personality traits, for instance – in other European thought the emphasis is on what one has yet to become (Pilgrim and Treacher 1992, Ryle 1997). I think this is underestimated in ageing. Liz Fawkes talked about how therapy may be one way of introducing a new form of mediation into old age so that, from a Vygotskian point of view, revolutions in thinking can occur (Sutton and Fawkes 2000). The stability of personality traits typically found in studies of ageing (Coleman 1999) could be partly because no new form of mediation has occurred. For instance, in their study of vital involvement in old age, Erikson *et al.* (1986) noted that:

Our subjects spoke clearly and interestingly about their lives, not seeming to hold back. When, however, we later learned about some of the crises they had met, the major challenges they had faced with their children and one another, we marvelled at the quiet, rather bland way in which they had presented their experiences to us, if they mentioned them at all. A number of times, a blanket statement quietly covered years of problematic relationships: 'There have been no problems with the children.' 'We have had no marital disagreements.' These family confrontations involved such traumatic experiences as the disabling effect of a child's illness and death, the extreme delinquency of an adolescent son or daughter, or marital discord that threatened divorce. We made little effort to draw out our informants on subjects they elected to bypass or treat as insignificant, since it was our goal to understand these people in terms of the conflicts they deemed important at this stage of their life and chose to discuss.

(p. 26)

My concern is that not drawing out what was bypassed or treated as insignificant repeats past neglects – a continued forgetting, of what is fore-gone (Sutton 1995). My concern is that this makes integration in late life more difficult, as if all is said and done. Talking recently with a client in her mid-seventies, she said to me that she had never thought of herself as 'traumatised' before; that she had thought that something was missing in her brain and that there was no hope for her now she was old. It was as though she had become resigned to being forgotten about as if there were no more to be said. Now, she said, she realises that 'It's not my brain. It's my mind', describing the shaming messages of her childhood and adulthood (and elderhood, as with 'you're past your sell-by date') as a kind of 'rote learning'. She said the difference to her now is the difference between saying to a child 'don't put your hands in the fire', and 'you'll survive'. She is now in her life literally giving new messages to her grandchildren and children which convey a sense of survival rather than fear. In Erikson's terms, she is renegotiating her adult lifestage of 'generativity', reshaping her caring for those she has produced and cared for in her life.

This client's words speak to the discourses of her time. 'Rote learning' was a recognised learning method, before the advent of computers. She was born into a time which then and before saw much mental disturbance that was biologically caused – birth trauma, thyroid deficiencies, syphilis and so on. I often hear older clients talking about their problems as something wrong with their 'brains'. Rather than this being a 'thinking error', it could be a kind of memory of the voices of those in their younger days. Talk of trauma is new; clients often mention Freud, but not Bowlby whose work on attachments would have been revolutionary in their younger years; and so on.

Knight (1999) cites research in the cognitive psychology of memory which shows that if cohort-specific words are used, some of the age differences in recall disappear. On the one hand this challenges traditional research which holds that older people's memories are worse than those of younger people. On the other hand, it makes it difficult to imagine the discontinuity and continuities of memory as meanings are renegotiated. It speaks to the same dilemma between memory as a faculty and memory in everyday life. For this client it is as if these new conversations have mediated a shift, from a discourse of 'brain' to one of 'minds'. For some clients it is as if they haven't had a chance to have these conversations. This is not to invalidate past conversations but to offer a different point of view from which new thinking becomes possible (Billig *et al.* 1988). Then a different relationship to one's past, present and future becomes possible. For Erikson this might be one way in which vital involvement in old age is renewed.

This potentially brings a different encounter with memory. The cognitive psychology of memory at present creates a peculiar disconnection between memory and affect, as though affect is not a part of memory; and a disconnection between memory and reminiscence (as 'pure' vs. 'practical' memory) which downplays reminiscence (Sutton 1995).

In the study of eye-witness testimony, for instance, the experimenter devises an experimental situation. Loftus and Burns (1982) showed two groups a video of a robbery. The experimental group also saw as part of the video a young boy being shot in the face. On subsequent testing, that group recalled fewer details of the event than the control group, and it was concluded that emotion interfered with recall of details of the event. In the experimental approach, the experimenter has defined what 'the event' is to be and also which parameters ('details of the event') to test for. The researched has no say in this. If the researched does not recall accordingly, then her/his memory can be judged as erroneous or flawed in some way.

Yet in experiencing the event of taking part in this research the feelings in seeing the young boy being shot may be central; the colour of the car or how fast it was going may not be. As Shotter (1990) says, affect *is* an aspect of practical embodied remembering. More than that, in this event of existence between researcher and researched, what the former registers with all their senses and beliefs is different from what the latter registers with all theirs. In the cognitive psychology of memory there is no attention to recall in terms of something someone said somewhere for some reason, in Middleton and Edwards's (1990) view. It is, they say, a 'single minded' approach.

Coles (1990) remarks that:

> When that tiny segment of society whom it is fashionable to refer to as social scientists attempt to study the process of memory and forgetting, issues of power and self-determination are rarely (I am tempted to say never) at issue. . . .
>
> Once the mind and memory are seen as extending beyond the 'individual skin' to encompass both the cultural milieu and the 'body politic', other dichotomies fall too. The notions that psychological content can be strictly separated from process, or that science can be strictly separated from history by its reliance on the experimental method, come in for pointed, sceptical scrutiny . . .
>
> In these new practices, issues of power and the self-determination of people(s) will no longer be cut off from scientific inquiry into memory.
>
> (Preface to Middleton and Edwards 1990, pp. viii, ix)

This disconnection of the current psychological science of memory from history can be viewed in its positioning of the study of autobiographical memory and reminiscence. Stuart-Hamilton (1994), for instance, discusses the experimental finding that, generally, older people give poorer-quality responses in autobiographical memory tests than younger people. For instance, they might say 'I remember going on a picnic when I was a child' rather than 'I remember going on a picnic on Salisbury Plain for my seventh birthday' (p. 80). He then remarks,

> Moving away from considerations of qualities of autobiograph-

ical memories, it is worth noting that reminiscence can have a therapeutic effect. Some commentators believe that 'reminiscence therapy' for the elderly should be encouraged, since it enables them to come to terms with their lives before they die.

(p. 80)

Here the experimental rationale of objectivity and measurement is used as a marker of the validity of remembering, which in a subtle way invalidates the authenticity of reminiscence (Sutton 1995). In the event, it is astonishing that issues of one's life and death can be taken as somehow outside the considerations of the qualities of autobiographical memory when older people have the longest memories of all.

Part of the problem is, as Donald (1991) points out, that 'memory' has been stored extra-corporeally for so long now – from hieroglyphs, to books, to computers – that it is easily conflated with information. Stiles (1997) suggests that the psychological residue of events is more properly characterised as a kind of 'voice' than a book or file to be processed and retrieved. This includes, I would suggest, memory for the 'event of existence', in Bakhtin's thought (Holquist 1990). This brings a different root metaphor for autobiographical memory: that is, from that of storage and retrieval, to that of the novel.

Novelness in therapy in old age

Peter Coleman (1999) discusses research which shows that by late life the life history report is a significant indicator of well-being. He points out, though, that not everyone in late life achieves a sense of having a story to tell – for instance, women whose stories are more fragmented, less integrated, with a sense of being objects of men's feelings rather than subjects in their own lives:

Some older people do not have a sense of having lived a 'life', but rather feel confused, hurt or depressed about what has happened to them. A satisfactory identity has not yet been constructed. Older as well as younger people may still need to find out who they are, and to begin composing a story they can call their own.

(Coleman 1999, p. 60)

The question is *how*; how can the person be helped to find out who they are and to begin composing a story they can call their own?

Elizabeth

Elizabeth was in her mid-seventies when she was referred for therapy because of her bipolar affective disorder, finding the roller-coaster of her emotions wearing and undermining. The referrer wasn't sure whether she would come to therapy because when well she would want to go it alone and when unwell she would take to bed and not come to the unit.

I became used to Elizabeth's 'mood shifts' which were more than shifts in mood. She changed in mind and body. She could be either buoyant, saying all was well and she didn't need therapy, or deeply depressed, feeling in need of someone to take the helm, only to drift, convinced she was lazy and undeserving of help. What was not being named was how either way she could not connect with me. I felt she had a profound mistrust in people. It was as though this part of her had no voice.

In her early sessions, in muted euphoria she talked of the wonder of her childhood. I wondered why she needed to be there with me. Later, she said to me unexpectedly that she had failed her school certificate in her first boarding school because the teachers weren't good, but she had passed it in the second because the teachers were very good. I asked her what made the first teachers not good and the second very good. She said it was the 'one-to-one'. In her second school she was amongst the few not to be evacuated, and so there was a high teacher-to-pupil ratio, which meant she could catch up and she passed. In her first school she said they never made allowances for her disrupted education (she moved around between relatives) and so she was unable ever to catch up and failed.

It occurred to me that if someone has lived in a culture, a society, a family that didn't make allowances, then all you have got to account for when things start to fail is yourself – so depression becomes possible. I put this to Elizabeth. She quietened. I thought she was going to cry, but she didn't. In a later session she said that, when she was young, her parents were always expecting compliance; that they still do. It was never said, she said, but it was there. I said that in this place there seems no place for feelings. On her psychotherapy file (a CAT tool which is a questionnaire about one's patterns of relating, not only to others but also to oneself in one's inner world, Ryle 1997) she indicated that sometimes to cope with confusing feelings she blanks off and becomes emotionally distant.

Elizabeth mentioned that her father believed that women should work and he decided that she should go into teacher training. She went, even though she didn't want to be a teacher. She stayed the course as her father advised but as soon as she finished she married – a successful businessman. Her rebellious side was falling into place. It was as though it was only in her rebelling that she felt alive, making euphoria possible. I have said to her that this is her fiery side – her 'hot' side like the hot countries she would love to go to. She replied that 'That's how I've survived, Laura.' Yet it has been a lonely (self-sufficient) survival with little bedrock to anchor in.

When she is low she can see no good in herself. It is like a near total eclipse of the sun. I introduced her to a Sanskrit word: 'dukha'. 'Dukha' conveys a sense of painful restriction, not physical, mental or emotional but all of these (Feuerstein 1990). She looked at me and quietened again. I am learning from Elizabeth that it is at these times, when neither of us has words, that she is prepared to think with me. At these times, I hear a different voice from Elizabeth. It is a distant and cautious voice, as she whispers that she used to lie on her bed as a child worrying about the spectre of war. At one point she voiced, 'How can a mother be so distant from her daughter?' I didn't know if she meant from her mother to her or from her to her daughter.

I feel her trust at these times and her vulnerability, risking the hope of a response that is not damaging. In CAT it is important always to keep a reciprocal awareness and not reciprocate past damaging patterns. I sense that for Elizabeth she has known too often another in a critical state or not attending when she is in anguish. She said that she wants to be able to cry but can't because this would be being a 'cry baby'. She has often used this phrase which in the English language is pejorative. I asked her about the child-rearing practices of her day. She said that then it was considered best to leave babies crying so as not to spoil them. It is as though she has learned that culturally the appropriate response to crying is not to attend. So she cannot know how to attend to her own silent crying. I have affirmed with her that crying doesn't hurt, it is the pejoratives ('cry baby') that do.

It seems to me that if Elizabeth can learn to be firm with her rebellious side and make allowances for herself unashamedly then she will be giving herself what she never had, namely adequate containment ('anchoring') as an adolescent and adequate nurturing as a child as an evacuee of war and survivor of boarding school. Then she will I think, experience what it is like to be 'safe within oneself', that is, a 'self-process' of relating safely from oneself to oneself. I think that this will bring her to a different position from which to view her self and her life, which may help her view her family and their stories in a different way. Then she may be able to imagine, and so start to create, a different-enough ending to her story with them and so be active in a vital way in how she will be remembered by her family for their futures (Erikson *et al.* 1986).

Thus, Elizabeth's despair and disconnection are partly 'existential'. In the 'event of her existence' (she in relation to others) she was born into narratives of unsaid expecting, where aliveness was by definition in rebelling; narratives which gave her little foundation for relating authentically to another in trust. It is as if she had to sustain herself on crumbs, in an emotional subsistence. The question then is, 'Who is the author of all this?'

Author[ess]ing in existence

Elizabeth reminds me of a song by a modern pop group, 'Mike and the Mechanics', called 'The Living Years'. The singer sings that he was held hostage to his father's hopes and fears, and that he wished he could have told him in the living years. I said to Elizabeth that it is as though she is held hostage even now to her parents' hopes and fears and that I wondered how far back that goes. She has told me about her tough aunts, how so many women were left on their own after World War I, so many men dying, that they had to take in the children. As she tells me more of the highs and lows of her life and those of her family past and present she as a woman is coming into view.

Elizabeth said to me once that the strange thing about being old is that there is no one to be accountable to any more. I have asked her whether she might account to herself from herself now; that is, become her own authority – to 'author her own existence' – now, so that (re)storying becomes possible. Then she may be in a position to experience herself as the subject in her own life, and her parents and children as subjects in theirs – metaphorically, able to have a different conversation with them in her living memory. Indeed, at times

Elizabeth is now more like a grandmother telling me her story; she is becoming 'generative' as she and her story unfold.

Coleman (1999) cites McAdams:

> Once the individual becomes a historian of the self, the history and the history making expand to encompass as much as they can. Generativity therefore becomes part of identity. In order to know who I am, I must have some inkling of what I have done and what I am going to do in order to be generative.
>
> (Coleman 1999, p. 59)

There is no 'other' person in this account. It is an account of an individual. Bakhtin might say it is a lonely account. Bakhtin talks about the completion of life, and how we need the other to complete us – I can see what is around you and you can do that for me. Indeed, his assertion is that abuse is an abuse of this 'excess of seeing', to say in effect 'stay in your solitude – there is no other for you' (Holquist and Liapunov 1990). In other words, a person 'cannot not-relate': in Bakhtin's thought there is 'nothing in itself'. Holquist explains that for Bakhtin:

> The tripartite nature of dialogue [self *and* other *and* relation] bears with it the seeds of hope : insofar as my 'I' is dialogic, it insures that my existence is not a lonely event . . . For in later times, and in other places, there will always be other configurations of such relations, and in conjunction with *that* other, my self will be differently understood . . . all have been correct to hope that outside the tyranny of the present there is a possible addressee who will understand them.
>
> There is neither a first word nor a last word. The contexts of dialogues are without limit. They extend into the deepest past and the most distant future. Even meanings born in dialogues of the remotest past will never be grasped once and for all . . . for nothing is absolutely dead: every meaning shall someday have its homecoming festival.
>
> (1990, pp. 38, 39)

Coleman (1996) says that although physical ageing is a hard fact it is not the only position from which to view ageing. A dialogic view offers a potential view across the lifespan, in the early forming in childhood, the formative adult years and the final forming in elderhood, in dialogue before and after life. From this perspective, the lifespan is viewed not so much as part of the natural order, but as part of the 'humanly produced order', so constituting not a closed 'text' but a text that is open to revision and reinterpretation (Coleman, 1999, p. 55), as a potential contribution to a developmental theory over a lifetime.

In the end, Coleman (1999) notes that it may be possible to move beyond storying as some older people are able to live without the more appropriative aspects of the self; and I am reminded of Lilian's faith and Elizabeth's fire which helped them to survive in ways impossible to quantify and describe.

Acknowledgements

I would like to thank 'Lilian' and 'Elizabeth' for their kind permission to publish their contributions to this chapter, presented anonymously and with some alterations in detail in order to further protect anonymity. I would also like to thank Dr Anthony Ryle and Professor Peter Coleman for commenting on previous drafts of this paper.

References

Beck, A.T. (1976/1989) *Cognitive Therapy and the Emotional Disorders*, London: Penguin Books.
Billig, M., Condor, S., Edwards, D., Gane, M., Middleton, D. and Radley, A. (1988) *Idealogical Dilemmas: A Social Psychology of Everyday Thinking*, London: Sage.
Britton, P.G. and Woods, R.T. (1999) 'Introduction', in R.T. Woods (ed.) *Psychological Problems of Ageing, Assessment, Treatment and Care*, Chichester: Wiley.
Burman, E. and Parker, I. (eds) (1993) *Discourse Analytic Research Repertoires and Readings of Texts in Action*, London: Routledge.
Coleman, P.G. (1996) 'Last scene of all?' Inaugural address as Professor of Psychogerontology, University of Southampton, UK.
Coleman, P.G. (1999) 'Identity management in later life', in R.T. Woods (ed.) *Psychological Problems of Ageing, Assessment, Treatment and Care*, Chichester: Wiley.
Coles, M. (1990) 'Preface' to D. Middleton and D. Edwards (eds) *Collective Remembering*, London: Sage.
Dick, L.P., Gallagher-Thompson, D. and Thompson, L.W. (1999)

'Cognitive-behavioural therapy', in R.T. Woods (ed.) *Psychological Problems of Ageing, Assessment, Treatment and Care*, Chichester: Wiley.

Donald, M. (1991) *Origins of the Modern Mind*, Cambridge, Mass.: Harvard University Press.

Erikson, E. (1950/1963) *Childhood and Society*, 2nd edn, New York: Norton.

Erikson, E.H., Erikson, J. and Kivnich, H.W. (1986) *Vital Involvements in Old Age*, New York: Norton.

Feuerstein, G. (1990) *Encyclopedic Dictionary of Yoga*, London: Unwin.

Freeman, M. (1993) *Rewriting the Self History Memory Narrative*, London: Routledge.

Gruneberg, M. and Morris, P. (1992) *Aspects of Memory, Vol. I: The Practical Aspects*, 2nd edn, London: Routledge.

Holquist, M. (1990) *Dialogism, Bakhtin and his World*, London: Routledge.

Holquist, M. and Liapunov, V. (1990) *Art and Answerability. Early Philosophical Essays by MM Bakhtin*, Austin: University of Texas Press.

Knight, B.G. (1996) *Psychotherapy with the Older Adult*, 2nd edn, Thousand Oaks, Calif.: Sage.

Knight, B.G. (1999) 'Psychodynamic therapy and scientific gerontology', in R.T. Woods (ed.) *Psychological Problems of Ageing, Assessment, Treatment and Care*, Chichester: Wiley.

Loftus, E.F. and Burns, T.E. (1982) 'Mental shock can produce retrograde amnesia', *Memory and Cognition*, 10, 318–323.

Margison, F. (2000) 'Cognitive analytic therapy: a case study in treatment development', *British Journal of Medical Psychology*, 73, 145–150.

Middleton, D. and Edwards, D. (eds) (1990) *Collective Remembering*, London: Sage.

Murphy, S. (2000) 'Provision of psychotherapy services for older people', *Psychiatric Bulletin*, 24, 181–184.

Neisser, U. (1978) 'Memory: what are the important questions?' in M.M. Gruneberg, P.E. Morris and R.N. Sykes (eds) *Practical Aspects of Memory*, London: Academic Press.

Pilgrim, D. and Treacher, A. (1992) *Clinical Psychology Observed*, London: Tavistock/Routledge.

Ryle, A. (1994) 'Projective identification – a particular form of reciprocal role procedure', *British Journal of Medical Psychology*, 67, 107–114.

Ryle, A. (1997) *Cognitive Analytic Therapy and Borderline Personality Disorders. The Model and the Method*, Chichester: Wiley.

Salkovskis, P.M. and Kirk, J. (1989) 'Obsessional Disorders', in K. Hawton, P.M. Salkovskis, J. Kirk and D. Clark. *Cognitive Behaviour Therapy for Psychiatric Problems*, Oxford: Oxford University Press.

Shotter, J. (1990) 'The social construction of remembering and forgetting', in D. Middleton and D. Edwards (eds) *Collective Remembering*, London: Sage.

Stiles, W.B. (1997) 'Signs and voices joining a conversation in progress', *British Journal of Medical Psychology*, 70, 169–176.

Still, A. and Costall, A. (1991) *Against Cognitivism. Alternative Foundations for Cognitive Psychology*, New York: Harvester Wheatsheaf.

Stuart-Hamilton, I. (1994) *The Psychology of Ageing*, 2nd edn, London: Jessica Kingsley.

Sutton, L.J. (1995) 'Whose memory is it anyway? A discursive critique of memory, depression and dementia in psychology'. Unpublished Ph.D. thesis, University of Southampton, UK.

Sutton, L.J. and Fawkes, L. (2000) 'No final word: Vygotsky and Bakhtin in CAT and Late Life', Presentation to the Annual CAT Conference, Guy's Hospital, London.

Chapter 2

Psychodynamic therapy

Mark Ardern

Historical background

The history of psychodynamic therapy is rooted in the founding of psychoanalysis by Sigmund Freud. It is therefore around a hundred years old. With a few notable exceptions the application of psychodynamic therapy to older people has developed within a single generation. A frequently cited reason for this is that Freud viewed psychoanalysis as unsuitable for patients over the age of 50 (Freud 1905). Consequently until the mid-1980s the Institute of Psycho-analysis rejected potential trainees who were more than 40 years of age. It is probable, however, that Freud's own stance on this would have been different had he been alive in a time when old age is of increasing preoccupation to western society. Karl Abraham, one of Freud's contemporaries, appears to have been exceptional in daring to apply psychoanalysis to older (i.e. late-middle-aged) people. He was surprised to find that these ventures counted among his most successful treatment outcomes, concluding that 'the age of the neurosis is more important than the age of the patient' (Abraham 1919).

Between the wars, Carl Jung, Freud's pupil turned rival, showed some interest in the analysis of older people, pointing out that mental activity continues to change throughout life. He stated that a successful adaptation to ageing depended upon 'an acceptance of what has and has not been achieved' (Jung 1931). Subsequently Erik Erikson produced his classification of the seven ages of man in which he indicated that life's journey culminated in the final phase which he termed 'integrity versus despair' (Erikson 1966). Elliot Jaques coined the now everyday term, the 'mid-life crisis'. He drew attention to some defensive manoeuvres middle-aged people (especially men) use to counteract their awareness of failing prowess (Jaques 1965).

By the 1970s psychoanalysis with very old people was becoming the subject of some curiosity. In Britain, Pearl King published her influential works in which she delineated common anxieties of ageing people. These are listed as various losses and threats of loss (King 1974, 1980). From the United States, in particular Boston, there has emerged an array of literature on both psychoanalysis and psychodynamic therapy with older people (see, for example, Duffy 1999). Although British interest has been characteristically more hesitant, several authors have added to our understanding of the dynamics between older patients and institutions that have the task of helping them (Martindale 1989, Porter 1997, Terry 1997).

The relationship between psychiatry and psychodynamic therapy has, by and large, not been one of interaction. Old age psychiatry, itself a new offspring of psychiatry, was formally recognised as a specialty in the UK in 1990. Its own development arose from the closure of large psychiatric hospitals and the move towards 'community care'. Studies had demonstrated that old people with concomitant psychiatric and physical illness were too often misplaced in either psychiatric or geriatric (medical) wards. This was shown to have an adverse effect on mortality. UK governmental policy in the 1970s strove to move psychiatric assessment units for older people away from remote asylums into district general hospitals in close approximation to departments of geriatric medicine. Some merged to become generic departments of healthcare of the elderly, most famously in Nottingham.

Old age psychiatry was, and still is, faced with two major clinical disorders – depression and dementia. Until now, old age psychiatric teams have largely concerned themselves with the detection and management of these conditions. The discovery of new medications, even 'anti-dementia' drugs, has justifiably encouraged a belief that physical treatments are able to 'cure' an increasing number of mentally ill older people. The future, perhaps in the field of gene therapy, is open to exciting possibilities. Despite (or perhaps because of) these preoccupations, and the fact that severe depression and dementia are not obvious conditions suitable for psychodynamic therapy, old age psychiatry has only just begun to incorporate psychodynamic thinking into its everyday work. Although a recent survey of psychotherapy departments indicates a continuing reluctance to take on older patients (Murphy 2000), some psychotherapists have become actively engaged in old age psychiatry teams (Garner 1999). Construction on the bridge between old age psychiatry and psychotherapy has therefore begun. With it comes the potential for additional or alternative treatments where medication and social manipulation alone are not enough.

Theoretical model

The term 'psychodynamic' suggests a process of interaction within and between the patient and therapist. The aim of psychodynamic therapy is to release the patient from neurotic conflicts, which may be producing both symptoms and difficulties in interpersonal relationships. Since nowadays we have more efficient treatments for neurotic symptoms (for example, medication or cognitive/behavioural therapies), psychodynamic therapy is targeted at relationship problems. Psychodynamic therapy strives to develop emotional maturation – individuals becoming more able to relate in an adult way rather than in an immature, conflicted way. Chronological age and intellectual age are poorly correlated with emotional age. This means that even a 70-year-old professor can still feel and behave like a lost little child. Psychodynamic therapy therefore facilitates the attainment of wisdom – that elusive prize we seek, as we grow older. Not surprisingly it takes longer to acquire wisdom than to be rid of neurotic symptoms. The matter of 'how long?' bedevils research in the field and is the source of considerable academic anguish.

Classical psychoanalysis involves 50-minute sessions up to five times a week, for several years. It is labour-intensive, expensive and can be a painful process. Hardly anyone, apart from trainee analysts themselves, has the time, money or motivation to engage in psychological treatment at this intensity. Long-term psychodynamic therapy is more modest. Within the National Health Service (NHS) in the UK some patients may be lucky enough to be offered an hour a week for a year. Inevitably the aims are more focused, and in 'brief' therapies (as few as six sessions) a specific difficulty such as grief or a marital problem is selected. Generally speaking the briefer the therapy the more the aim is repair work rather than fundamental personality change.

Although psychoanalysis and psychodynamic therapy have undergone considerable diversification, both are underpinned with common principles. The age of the patient does not alter these principles. However, as we shall see later, their practice may have to be modified when working with older people. The components of psychodynamic therapy are now discussed in some detail.

The unconscious mind

Not all human behaviour makes sense or is rationally determined, and the unconscious mind is a powerful force operating in each of us. According to psychodynamic theory, only by uncovering unconscious processes can we begin to throw light on why we behave as we do; and more particularly reveal why some people seem to end up repeating their mistakes.

Freud's discovery of the unconscious mind came about as he was attending lectures on hysteria. Towards the end of the nineteenth century, hysteria was a condition of great interest to neurologists. One of these, Charcot, was producing dramatic results. In a series of clinical demonstrations to his audience of neurologists (which included Freud), Charcot successfully rid patients of hysterical symptoms by means of a new treatment known as hypnosis. Freud, having become fascinated with the reasons for Charcot's success, hypothesised that symptoms represented the expression of a psychic conflict in the patient. He believed that the patient had unconsciously repressed previous trauma, and that the symptoms symbolised this trauma in a way that was culturally acceptable. Freud's view was that the psychic conflict was related to unwanted sexual urges; from this he later developed his notion of the Oedipus Conflict. Freud speculated that cure of the patient's symptoms depended upon a relationship that arose in the treatment. He believed that a suggestible patient, literally in the hands of a powerful, charismatic doctor, awakened a memory of an earlier relationship (unbeknown to either patient or doctor); that is, the patient's internalised parental figures are now re-enacted in the therapeutic drama.

To test his hypothesis Freud embarked on a modification of the hypnotic technique. Rather then standing over his patient, he chose to sit quietly behind the patient out of sight. With the patient lying on a couch he merely asked his patient to report whatever entered his mind, however seemingly foolish or embarrassing. Freud called this technique **free association**. Straightforward enough as this request appears, in practice it proves exceedingly difficult for patients to comply. Routinely patients will stumble, fall silent or change subject. Freud concluded that all patients asked to 'free associate' exhibit an unconscious **resistance**. In other words, although a patient consciously strives to cooperate (in order to be cured), the unconscious mind fights to maintain the familiar safety of the status quo.

Over time, Freud observed that patients undergoing psychoanalysis behaved towards him in irrational and startling ways. For example, a patient might declare extraordinary feelings of annoyance or adoration. Since Freud was (and modern-day therapists are) careful not to contaminate the sessions with judgements or personal disclosures he concluded that the patient's inexplicable attitudes were based on projections arising from the patient's unconscious. Fantasies, in the forms of hopes and fears, become located in the therapist, most commonly the therapist being attributed with parental qualities based on the patient's previous experience. Freud termed this phenomenon of attribution the **transference**. The reverse phenomenon, the **countertransference**, is the feelings generated in the therapist by the patient. Nowadays psychodynamic therapists place particular importance on monitoring countertransference feelings in themselves in order to learn about their patient.

Since the therapist's own resistances and complexes (and personality) provide a limitation on what can be discovered about the patient in therapy, psychodynamic therapists are required to undertake their own personal therapy. In this way, the therapist becomes more able to move toward a position of relative objectivity, and less likely to spoil the treatment with his own personal agenda.

As with Freud, modern psychodynamic therapy encourages the patient to speak his mind as freely as he is able. The therapist's task is to watch, listen and (by way of observing the transference and countertransference) try to piece together the jigsaw of the patients' internal world. Other evidence for unconscious mental activity can sometimes be seen in patients' slips of the tongue ('parapraxes') and the reporting of dreams; the latter Freud called 'the Royal Road to the Unconscious'.

In assessing patients for their suitability for psychodynamic therapy, therapists do have to ask questions. Not least there is the need to gather a certain amount of history and to seek clarification of what the patient is attempting to communicate. The main therapeutic comments from the therapist, however, are interpretations. The aim of interpretation is to bring to conscious awareness that which is unconscious to the patient. A patient who has anxieties about authority figures – for example, being too eager to please for fear of being slapped down – will recreate this in his transference towards the therapist. Here the therapist is invested with the same potential to humiliate the patient. At some point the therapist will need to interpret the patient's timidity, without alienating the patient. The timing of interpretations is therefore a crucial test of the therapist's expertise. Inexperienced therapists tend to make rash interpretations based on little evidence (what Freud termed 'wild analysis'). Patients who have armour-plated defences will deflect even correct interpretations as nonsense. The art of interpretation undertaken skilfully with a receptive patient will enable a dawning of **insight** into the patient's way of relating. Although sudden and dramatic insights do sometimes occur, and accompanied by the release of emotion (catharsis), interpretations are more commonly used to reveal the patient's defensive structure. Assuming that interpretations are made in a way that the patient can digest, there develops a deepening of the so-called 'therapeutic alliance'. This gives courage to patients' exploration of hitherto carefully guarded secrets. Mature therapy then becomes a shared discovery rather than a power struggle. A parody of psychodynamic therapy is that a therapist does nothing apart from offer knowing grunts to a patient lying confused and frustrated on a couch.

Since Freud's day the evolution of psychodynamic therapy has resulted in various modifications of therapy and practice. Melanie Klein was the first to analyse children (see Segal 1964). Klein observed that children at play unconsciously enact conflicts in relation to parents, teachers and siblings. She used her patient's drawings to reflect with her child-patient about his inner mental world. In contrast to Freud, who focused on the first five years of life as of primary importance in the development of neurosis, Klein believed that the origins of neurosis stem from infancy. She believed that an infant's successful individuation from the maternal breast involves a move from its view of the outside world as persecutory. At the earliest psychic phase an infant has no conception of being separate from the breast. Gradually it realises that this source of nourishment is not constant but depends on factors external to itself. A breast which gives milk freely is benign, but a breast which is withheld is perceived as persecuting (Klein's so-called **paranoid schizoid position**). The infant therefore feels vulnerable to the apparent whims of the breast beyond its control. In revenge it fantasises attacks on the unyielding breast. When the breast nevertheless continues to be offered the infant begins to realise its own potential for destructive retaliation. During this second phase (the **depressive position**) the infant's capacity for guilt is developed. Klein believed that this assimilation is central to an adult's ability to simultaneously hold opposing concepts in mind. In other words psychologically healthy adults do not split the world into 'good' and 'bad' (as in fairy stories); rather, relationships with others involve an appreciation of wholeness and a need to compromise.

Extensions of the views of Freud and Klein have continued to emphasise the importance of adequate parenting in the development of personality. Satisfactory relationships in adult life depend at least in part on solid early foundations (for example, Winnicott 1958, Balint 1968 and Bowlby 1979). A secure early attachment to a 'good enough' mother (who is attentive to the needs of her child, without being anxiously fussy or neglectful) will result in the development of the child's internalised sense of trust. In adult life, and particularly in times of emotional upset, a person is able to draw upon this investment, and is thereby less vulnerable to psychological breakdown. This 'attachment theory' implies that the psychodynamic therapist offers a symbolic reparenting. The therapist offers himself to help the patient with unswerving attention in a way that mirrors a parent's positive regard for his child.

Contemporary psychodynamic therapy weaves together concepts such as these. Although therapists will receive their training in a predominant model (e.g. Freudian, Kleinian or Jungian), it is likely that they will also develop a style that befits their own personality. Regardless of differences in approach, all psychodynamic therapists believe in three common principles. They are:

1   The importance of the unconscious mind.
2   The phenomena of transference and countertransference.
3   The use of interpretation.

Before we leave the model, it is necessary to return to Freud's notion of defences (Freud 1966). All of us need psychological defences if we are to survive. Problems only develop when these mechanisms are used excessively or inappropriately. A useful example of the mobilisation of defences occurs in the face of bereavement. Our universal reaction to hearing the news of the death of someone close to us is to experience **denial**. This is manifested by statements such as 'it can't be true . . . I don't believe it'.

Rapidly this becomes overtaken by feelings of numbness or unreality (**dissociation**). In turn, the numbness may be replaced with conflicting feelings of anger, yearning, regret and sadness. The dynamics of grief give evidence of the mind's attempts to mobilise defences against total psychological collapse. In the early phase of grief, denial and dissociation are defensively erected to ward off overwhelming anxiety. In pathological grief reactions, one or more of these defences can become cemented in place, blocking the road to mourning. For example, the person may refuse to accept the reality of his loss for months or years, rather than minutes. An alternative manifestation of pathological grief is clinical depression (what Freud called 'melancholia'). Here life itself does not seem possible in the absence of the other.

Since defence mechanisms are constructed in early life their relative interplay is present in childhood but becomes modified with the maturation of character. In fact they define character. Numerous defence mechanisms have been described, some apparently more primitive than others. **Splitting** and **projective identification** were ones coined by Klein. She would have viewed patients with an excessively paranoid view of the world as having never developed the capacity for self-criticism – blame therefore being located in others. Although this offers protection, it usually brings the person into conflict with others, reinforcing persecutory feelings. Klein also described **manic defences** in which omnipotent control of the environment serves to avoid despair.

Rationalisation attempts to manage dangerous emotions with intellectual argument. For example, if we fail in a job application our rationalisation might be 'I never wanted that job anyway'. Rationalisation is synonymous with the expression 'sour grapes'. **Sublimation** is regarded as a relatively sophisticated mechanism in which internal psychic conflicts are harnessed to creativity. For example, artists or musicians use sublimation to channel these conflicts into productive work. Many other defence mechanisms have been delineated (see, for example, Anna Freud 1966); and no doubt some remain to be 'discovered'.

Since defence mechanisms are unconscious, they are not ours to control any more than we can change our personalities at will. Psychodynamic therapy, however, attempts to map out personal defensive structures and reflect these back to the patient. Primitive and unhelpful defences thereby become replaced by more constructive ones.

In summary, psychodynamic therapy involves a relationship that is cultivated between the patient and therapist. The psychodynamic therapist uses his formulation from knowledge of the patient's early life and reports of the patient's *modus operandi* in his everyday life. Within the therapeutic relationship further evidence is gathered from the patient's transference reactions and the therapist's own countertransference reactions towards the patient. The tool of interpretation is combined with the patient's new experience of a trusting, containing and reflecting therapist who unconditionally offers help in the absence of judgement.

Applications of psychodynamic therapy and selection of patients

Generally speaking, a patient considered potentially suitable for psychodynamic therapy will need to fulfil the following criteria. The patient:

1   Should demonstrate some awareness that neurotic symptoms have *meaning*.
2   Is motivated to *change*.
3   Accepts a degree of personal *responsibility*.
4   Will be able to tolerate and digest *interpretation*.
5   Is realistic about the fact that this form of treatment requires *time*.

From these basic principles it can be seen that many people, of whatever age, are not candidates for psychodynamic therapy:

1   Psychosis is usually regarded as a contraindication. The loss of contact with reality exposes the patient to making dangerous misinterpretations of the process. In particular the patient is likely to develop a malignant form of transference where the therapist automatically becomes the persecutor.
2   Severe depression with excessive preoccupations of unworthiness, guilt or despair requires a more supportive approach (in addition to other forms of management). No amount of talking will rescue a patient who has regressed to the position of refusing to eat or drink. Psychodynamic therapy may even exacerbate profoundly depressive thinking.
3   Limited intelligence precludes the possibility of abstract

thinking and the use of metaphor. This restricts the patient's appreciation of the therapist's behaviour other than in a concrete way.

4   Markedly obsessional characters may initially give the semblance of cooperation (for example, by way of punctuality) but can be expected to develop a combative rivalry with the therapist's perceived power.

5   Extreme narcissism will lead to domination of therapy by the patient's need to be adored. Interpretations are unlikely to be welcomed, so that early infatuation with the therapist will change to denigration once the patient's idealising fantasies are not realised.

6   Sociopathic (psychopathic) individuals are unsuitable by way of little capacity for guilt or self-reflection. These persons' intolerance of a necessary degree of frustration frequently leads to violent 'acting out'.

7   The concomitant misuse of alcohol or drugs allows the patient to avoid unbearable realities. As these substances are used recreationally to blot out unwanted feelings (such as inhibitions), people who depend upon drugs find psychodynamic therapy difficult.

8   Finally, significant cognitive impairment (dementia) will hinder the retention and processing that therapy demands.

Psychiatry, politics and the law struggle with the controversial term 'personality disorder'. Its relevance to psychodynamic therapy is implied from some of the features just delineated, and will determine whether therapists offer this form of treatment. Personality disorder is widely agreed to be conceptually different from mental illness. However, in describing personality, the distinction between what is normal and what is pathological undoubtedly varies with the prevailing trends and culture of the day. Despite the term's pejorative overtones of moral degeneracy, philosophers might point out that all humans could be considered as having problems with aspects of their personalities. For example, what works well (in terms of defence mechanisms) at age 40 may not do so at age 50.

Doctors describe personality disorders as: 'severe disturbances in the characterological constitution and behavioural tendencies of the individual . . . associated with considerable personal and social disruption' (ICD-10 1992). Personality disorder cannot be diagnosed until late adolescence, but is relatively enduring thereafter. It also (by way of a somewhat circular argument) implies poor treatability. Personality disorder could usefully be considered as a state of extreme emotional underdevelopment, arising from genetic factors and (significantly for psychotherapists) defective upbringing. Generally, people with marked personality disorders are not viewed as suitable for psychodynamic therapy. Certainly, individuals who operate primitive defence mechanisms are unlikely to be insightful enough to request it. Others may do so, but with little serious intent to change themselves. Finally there are people who give the convincing appearance of suitability, but unconsciously use therapy to settle old scores (see Storr 1979, for an honest account of therapeutic mistakes by an expert in the field).

There are, as always, exceptions to these exclusion criteria, notably in the realms of forensic psychotherapy. Nevertheless the troubled older person who has demonstrable interest and motivation to engage in psychodynamic therapy will more than likely be able to make use of it. Much has been made of the concept of 'psychological mindedness' as if it were a congenitally acquired talent. In fact most of us have to learn this skill; sometimes in therapy, but mostly just through living. Freud's supposed mental rigidity in older people has been exaggerated. In contrast to young people's tendency to act impulsively at the mercy of biological drives, older people are more likely to be reflective. A second argument sometimes promoted is that older people have 'no time in which to change'. Some psychotherapists, however, have found that an older person's appreciation of the finiteness of life acts as a useful catalyst to focus the patient on what might be possible in whatever time exists (Hildebrand 1986). This often provides a sense of urgency in attending to the resolution of conflicts.

Patients who have suffered psychiatric breakdown but have largely recovered may be sufficiently curious to understand 'why' they became ill, and more especially 'why now'. Thus psychodynamic therapy can be used as secondary prevention rather than cure, as one of the examples at the end of this chapter demonstrates. Psychodynamic therapy is neither achievable nor desirable in many clinical situations. This is especially so for severely disturbed patients referred to old age psychiatry departments. Nevertheless a psychodynamic understanding sheds further light on mysterious and taxing dilemmas where elderly people find themselves in emotional distress. Even those patients who have extensive brain disease present symptoms and behaviours which are coloured by personality make-up. Often the content of the patient's delusions betray old ghosts from the past, which are now reawakened in mental illness.

Despite potential suitability for a psychodynamic treatment approach some patients prefer to see the medical model as the answer to their problems. Others may be wary of talking treatments, especially those which (like psychodynamic therapy) require time, effort and no guarantee of benefit. The urgent life-threatening crises which befall elderly people may seem far too immediate to cultivate introspection. In later life a person's defence mechanisms will be threatened from the onslaught of various vicissitudes. Losses and the anticipation of future losses face all people in old age. The older person's ability to negotiate these will depend upon the robustness of his characterological make-up. Ideally, as previously indicated, psychodynamic therapists will select patients who genuinely seek to understand themselves better. In practice many older patients entering therapy will need to experience a taste of what is possible from psychodynamic therapy and, if they are to continue, some early benefits. In the first encounter between therapist and patient a trial interpretation will gauge the patient's receptiveness to this form of treatment. If correct, and accepted, it helps build the patient's optimism.

For situations in which, for one reason or another, psychodynamic therapy is not considered useful, many of the elements of this form of therapy can help staff to achieve a sense of purpose. Elderly patients in anguish are demanding on staff who in turn can feel overwhelmed and impotent. There is a potential for multidisciplinary teams to become split and fragmented – a process which threatens to undermine treatment plans (Gabbard 1989). In these situations staff can unconsciously enact their personal grievances on vulnerable patients, leading to malignant spirals of hopelessness. One of the benefits of employing an experienced psychodynamic therapist within a multidisciplinary team is to enhance staff cohesiveness. By this is meant not 'tea and sympathy' but a designated thinking space away from the heat of the clinical situation. This encourages a spirit of enquiry into and understanding of the dynamic processes at work. These processes operate in the patient, in organisations caring for them, and between the two. An example of the practical application of this would be the provision of psychodynamic workshops on a group basis. Staff of all ranks and from all disciplines bring examples of clinical problems. Depending on the willingness of the staff to risk disclosing their own (counter-transference) feelings towards patients it becomes possible to develop greater insight into a particular patient's way of relating. The resulting revelations for staff greatly enhance their capacity to contain the projections of their patients without reacting in a mindless way. The psychodynamic therapist thereby enables staff to embrace 'troublesome' patients more confidently. Such a theoretical framework underpins care plans whether or not psychological therapies form part of them (see, for example, Zagier Roberts 1994, Terry 1997).

Therapists who choose to work with patients in later life will have to modify selection criteria based on other realities, such as resources available. One decision is whether to offer individual or group therapy. Group psychodynamic therapy offers an opportunity for members to observe themselves in relation to others. In groups, transference phenomena can be seen in action between individual patients as well as towards the therapists. There are many factors that are considered therapeutic in the use of groups (see Yalom 1985). Possibly the most potent of these is that of universality – a sharing of common experience in a microcosm of a society. Practicalities may be more influential than theory in determining the value of group therapy. Some patients find groups less threatening than individual therapy whereas for others the reverse is the case. Commonly, patients may benefit from some individual therapy before they are ready to tolerate the competitive environment of others' distress.

Selecting patients for groups can be more difficult than for individual therapy. Although some psychodynamic groups aim to be more supportive than strictly analytical, an equivalent degree of psychological sophistication among members will reduce the chances of scape-goating and allow a group to progress cohesively. A recent paper (Canete *et al.* 2000) describes the use of psychodynamic group therapy with the elderly in an NHS out-patient setting.

Therapy in practice

Staff from a range of professional disciplines will provide most psychodynamic therapy with older patients in hospital care. With a basic understanding of the principles, even relatively inexperienced therapists may take on pre-selected patients, provided this is under the supervision of an experienced psychotherapist. It is not possible to overemphasise the importance of supervision. Many well-meaning but naïve staff wish to 'have a go'. However, psycho-dynamic therapy is different from simple supportive counselling. Since the former involves interactions which seek to foster and rec-reate powerful unconscious earlier relationships, unsupervised staff may find themselves on the receiving end of transference projections and unwittingly retaliate – to their patients' detriment. Although a trained psychotherapist will have acquired the skill of 'internal supervision' it is still usual for him to seek an external supervisor. This helps the therapist to develop a clearer view in which, so to say, he sees both the wood and the trees.

Supervision will therefore be primarily concerned with unravel-ling the complex dynamics that exist in the patient's internal world and how these relate to his external situation. The transferences which develop towards the therapist, being unconscious, must be understood in supervision. Equally the countertransference reac-tions provoked in the therapist require careful analysis. Particular emotional reactions can be anticipated when a younger therapist is undertaking therapy with an older patient. It might be assumed that an older patient will automatically come to see his younger therap-ist as a child or grandchild surrogate. However, transference spans the generations. A younger therapist can also be seen as having parental qualities – something which may come as an unwelcome surprise to him. The therapist may be viewed as well-intentioned, but this frequently conceals an older patient's concerns about the therapist's (in)competence. These so-called negative feelings in the transference are usually kept in check, since the older patient may unconsciously fear that his younger therapist will not be able to withstand such ungrateful expressions. Conversely, a younger ther-apist, who is typically struggling to aspire to greater autonomy and mastery (appropriate to his own time of life), may be too eager to gratify his patient's neediness.

Only in supervision may it be possible to uncover the therapist's own anxieties about being overwhelmed, and his own negative feel-ings towards the patient – all of which he too tries to keep away from conscious awareness. The success of dynamic psychotherapy will depend to a large extent upon whether the younger therapist has the capacity to tolerate and reflect upon these anxieties, both in supervision and ultimately with the patient. (For a vivid account of transference and countertransference processes in therapy with older patients, including case examples, see Newton and Jacobowitz 1999.)

One of the cardinal requirements in psychodynamic therapy is the importance of reliability, consistency and the maintenance of boundaries. Many older people entering therapy will have experienced problems with their own early life attachments. More recently they will also have encountered, or be facing, losses, a crucial one being the anticipated loss of independence. Older patients are often highly suspicious that healthcare professionals, however superficially caring, are secretly wishing to rid themselves of unbearable demands placed upon them. Staff may manifest their discomfort by various unconscious means – for example, cancelling appointments or intrusively promoting unwanted help. These common anxieties held by younger therapists in relation to older patients have been well described (Martindale 1989). At worst, therapists who rationalise that they are powerless to help may discharge patients precipitately. Negotiating termination (see later) and giving plenty of notice of holiday breaks are therefore especially important in work with older people.

In contrast to psychodynamic therapy with younger patients, therapists will find themselves faced with several additional considerations. Older patients are more likely to have multiple problems, which include physical ill health and increasing social isolation. While these are often matters at the heart of therapy, psychodynamic therapy walks a delicate balance between trying to uncover meaning (using interpretation) and acknowledging the limitations these difficulties place on the patient's life. Injudicious interpretation of physical symptoms may have the effect of belittling the patient's real problems. Social isolation (which may be self-imposed) is not the same as loneliness (the personal experience of the absence of significant others). An elderly person's fear of being abandoned or humiliated may not necessarily be a manifestation of neurosis, but may be an accurate observation of reality.

Unlike the rule with younger patients, a display of physical contact (for example, helping a patient up from a chair) may be necessary, so long as it is not undertaken to gratify the compulsive care-giving of the therapist. Since it arises not uncommonly, the offer of gifts from patients is perhaps more problematic than with younger patients. This powerful communication from the patient to the therapist may seem harmless enough. Although gifts can be a straightforward concretisation of gratitude, unconscious motives may be manipulation or expression of narcissistic wishes to be the therapist's favourite patient. Rejection of gifts is always hurtful, sometimes enough to terminate therapy altogether. A reasonable solution when placed 'on the spot' could be to temporarily accept the gift on condition that the therapist is permitted to use this as material for interpretation.

In the public sector, the environment within which therapy is conducted is often far from ideal. Sadly, finding a suitable space which can be guaranteed free from intrusion, week in, week out, can be difficult in a busy institution. No surgeon would agree to operate in a theatre that was contaminated or had inadequate lighting; nor would he permit telephone calls mid-operation. Similarly, the therapist's duty is to ensure that, as far as possible, reliability and sanctuary are maintained. On no account short of a catastrophe should the therapist leave the presence of the patient.

The therapist should arrange for a comfortable waiting area outside the therapy room (with a nearby toilet) and aim to arrive precisely at the appointed time. If the patient is late he should find the therapist there already. The therapist consistently greets the patient in a polite, courteous manner. In treatment sessions (although not during assessment), the therapist then remains silent and devotes himself to what Freud described as 'evenly suspended attention'. This is a complex technical procedure whereby the therapist observes not only the patient's manifest behaviour and utterances but his own associations. In the author's experience protracted silences are less common with older patients. More often the patient's anxiety may be evidenced by garrulousness.

Commonly, elderly patients will be taking medication. Where the therapist is medically qualified a desire to discuss medication may threaten to deflect the therapist from the task in hand. Ideally the therapist should not be the same person as the one who prescribes. Increasingly, however, psychodynamic therapists, and even psychoanalysts (Donovan and Roose 1995), have come to accept that concurrent psychiatric medication is not necessarily a drawback to therapy. In depression, medication helps with the so-called 'biological' symptoms (appetite, sleep, energy and concentration), while dynamic psychotherapy offers to throw light on meaning. Once the patient has responded to antidepressants she can usefully devote this new-found energy to working with the therapist. An analogy is that of using crutches to facilitate independent mobility. In time these supports may be dispensed with – a decision which should remain one negotiated between the patient and prescribing physician rather than with the psychotherapist.

Finally, a few words about termination in psychodynamic therapy. In brief (focal) therapy, the date of termination is usually decided from the outset. In longer-term therapies, and in the state sector especially, it may be determined by factors external to the wishes/needs of both the patient and therapist. As a metaphor for the finiteness of life, a major therapeutic activity will consist of negotiating the relinquishing of therapy. This is brought acutely into focus in a report of group psychotherapy for (now elderly) child Holocaust survivors (Tauber and Van der Hal 1998). There the primary psychological task for the group members was to tolerate the ending of the group – which inevitably provoked powerful memories of extermination. To a lesser degree all older people who are moving (with varying psychological success) towards a position of reduced autonomy will find termination problematic. So too may their therapists whose countertransference reactions are likely to include guilt. (In the Holocaust group the therapists found themselves delaying its termination.) For particularly troubled older patients, any notion of outliving the therapy may be intolerable. In these cases the decision to embark on indefinite, supportive therapy (such as that described at the end of this chapter) may be justified if psychiatric breakdown is anticipated. The matter of termination with older people is therefore one which requires particular consideration. Its timing and implementation will obviously depend upon the aims of the therapy, and the degree to which losses are navigable.

Case illustrations

I Long-term individual psychodynamic therapy

Mr Martin, a 63-year-old man presented with panic attacks during which he would summon an ambulance to the local Accident and Emergency department. Several years previously the patient had had a cardiac arrest and he continued to suffer from severely disabling coronary artery disease. The patient was well aware of the physiology of anxiety and its likeness to organic symptoms of heart disease. Worse than his fear of dying, he believed that he might collapse in the street in a humiliated state, with passers-by contemptuously stepping over him.

Immediately after his cardiac arrest he regained consciousness and found himself surrounded by the numerous doctors and nurses who had resuscitated him. He admitted that this undivided attention had been a unique experience in his life and recalling it gave him great pleasure. Subsequently he made special efforts to engage the consultant and nurses by calling them by their first names, cracking jokes and buying presents. Unconsciously Mr Martin wanted to make sure that he would, because of his life-threatening cardiac arrhythmias and charming personality, always be in the minds of the clinical team whenever he would need them again. He came to therapy ostensibly to find out more about his panic attacks.

Mr Martin had been brought up abroad in an orphanage and was clearly emotionally impoverished. He recalled being sexually abused by older boys at the orphanage and had engaged in some prostitution himself in his teens. Highly intelligent he later moved to drama school. Although he described himself as 'bi-sexual' he had managed a ten-year live-in relationship with a man much older than himself, whom he cared for during a long and protracted terminal illness. By his middle years, Mr Martin had attained considerable notoriety as an actor, was financially comfortable and had attracted quite a social circle, entertaining with dinner parties of which he was especially proud.

The panic attacks began as this semblance of togetherness began to crack. His mobility declined secondary to his heart disease, his partner died, and friends and acquaintances took less interest in him. Increasing isolation and relative poverty reminded him of his earlier abandonment. As his heart disease advanced, he strived for a special, almost personal, relationship with the Consultant Cardiologist who he hoped would rescue him. There had been some discussion of a heart transplant. His panic attacks/cardiac arrhythmias would repeatedly lead him to hospital, where he would obtain some solace in holding court with medical students – trying to be their favourite, most memorable patient.

Long-term individual psychotherapy (which lasted five years) was aimed at revealing to him insight into his narcissistic personality. An idealising transference towards the younger male therapist not surprisingly had an erotic component, but Mr Martin was able to voice his fantasies towards the therapist in a way that helped him distinguish between his different needs: between the emotional and physical and between the imagined and real. Mr Martin had never experienced unconditional love – only that linked with, as a youth, his good looks, then as a young man, his role as an actor, cook and raconteur, and now, as an ageing man, the image he promoted of considerable charm and medical interest. He even fantasised that his funeral would be quite special. Mr Martin longed for an elaborate and theatrical affair full of well-wishers.

The therapy had several aspects. One was to offer a unique experience of containment which did not depend on him performing in any particular way. The sessions actively encouraged his attachment towards the therapist and lessened his propensity to go unnecessarily to the Accident and Emergency department. In parallel the therapist and Mr Martin mutually examined his narcissistic craving. While he was skilled at engaging his cardiology team, an excessive use of manipulation threatened to drive potential medical help away. There were some signs that the cardiac team were becoming both bored and irritated with what they saw as 'crying wolf'. A long-term view of therapy was that of avoiding a catastrophic depressive breakdown (and possibly suicide).

The therapist was able to withstand the patient because of supervision which allowed ventilation of the complex transference and countertransference reactions. Mr Martin gradually came to realise his propensity to idealise and/or denigrate care-givers. In the final year of therapy, when the patient's breathlessness rendered him near immobile, and shortly before he suddenly died, the therapist acceded to the patient's non-neurotic and courageous request to continue with weekly sessions in the patient's own home. Mr Martin, though critical of some of his home care services, had been helped not to reject them. He did not become depressed; nor did he die alone.

2 Group therapy

A psychiatrist and a psychoanalyst set up a long-term out-patient group for older people. The aim was to help patients who had previously had severe depressive breakdowns avoid relapse. The means to this end was to encourage these patients to develop an awareness of the links between their quiescent psychiatric symptoms and their personal histories. For various reasons all of these patients had found themselves socially isolated and, in the face of old age, becoming increasingly fearful that their individual needs would not be met by the statutory services. One man, pampered as a child, now wished for an idealised care in which every whim could be anticipated and catered for. Another lady who lost all her relations in a Nazi death camp seemed puzzled as to why the young students she possessively invited to live with her all fled. A third man, having anxiety attacks, had been visited at home by a young female psychologist. Having developed a crush on her he longed that she would visit him regularly and in perpetuity.

All of the group members had ended up facing old age alone. They were terrified that their old age would be just as uncertain as their experiences in childhood. By making connections between these temporally dislocated anxieties the patients developed some awareness that their 'illnesses' were not random misfortunes, but understandable, and therefore potentially faceable. The transference reactions towards the two therapists mirrored the patients' own wishes from their past, and their current exaggerated belief that old people are inevitably neglected. Some of their coping mechanisms, in which they clung to whatever help was around, were discovered to be exacerbating their isolation. The patients rarely dared to challenge the therapists, worried that offended therapists might disband the group altogether. Any envious feelings towards the therapists' perceived good health, youth and financial security rarely surfaced openly.

In this group for extremely psychologically vulnerable people the therapists came to realise that the patients benefited less from clever interpretations, but more from the continued long-term existence of the group. It would be accurate to describe this particular group, though run on psychodynamic principles, as largely ego-supportive – one which complemented these patients' vulnerability to future relapse.

3 Psychodynamics in a ward setting

In this case psychodynamic understanding helped contain a psychiatric team struggling to help plan care for an elderly woman who tested their resolve.

Miss Patterson, now 75, had been brought up in a children's home. Her father had been in hospital with a probable depressive breakdown during her childhood. She then went to a convent school and moved to the soft furnishings department of a Birmingham department store where she remained until she retired. She was a woman of secretive, rather paranoid character who had never achieved personal intimacy.

Her first depressive psychosis had occurred ten years previously. Miss Patterson, having ceased work and following the death of an acquaintance, then had a series of admissions, punctuated with day hospital attendances. Her final admission was to a psychiatric ward where she was hostile and aggressive. She ran out of the ward to the police station reporting that she was a missing patient. She would hit staff, smash ornaments and generally cause mayhem. Staff debated the matter of how responsible she was for this behaviour. Many times the staff came to the conclusion that she was 'playing up'. In turn she was moved from ward to ward in order to rid the staff of her demands. Staff generally felt demoralised and guilty. Sometimes they were punitive.

The psychiatric team decided to meet every three months to identify and document their observations. They were encouraged to note their feelings, *even hatred* of the patient. These meetings helped to normalise the personal reactions of staff. They also began to make sense of why Miss Patterson, with her profound mistrust, reacted to institutions in such a regressed manner. Although the behaviour was 'attention seeking' it became possible to see also that behind this lay her terror of being neglected. Even abuse by staff, which the patient provoked, seemed better for the patient than being forgotten. The staff were gradually able to be helped to develop a sense of what it must be like to be Miss Patterson in a psychiatric ward. Individual sessions between Miss Patterson and a psychologist and art therapist confirmed the psychodynamic formulation. Staff felt more relaxed at limit-setting and less worried that they would be cruel in containing the patient. More constructive plans could then be devised with a longer-term vision. Gradually the patient developed confidence that she would not be discharged into a vacuum. She then visited nursing homes with members of staff whom she liked and her behaviour correspondingly improved.

Summary

Psychodynamic therapy is no longer restricted to the young. Developmental issues arising in the latter part of life often covertly resonate with those of the older person's formative years. If we are to understand the individual predicament facing each of our older patients, we need to actively uncover links between today's distress and yesterday's trauma. Older people's hopes and fears will inevitably become located in younger health professionals whom they encounter. Conversely young therapists may find the experience of their older patients' demands troubling, itself a reason for attention. Unlike in other psychological treatments, psychodynamic therapists deliberately foster and examine these interactions. While many older patients, by way of the severity of their disturbance, will not be suitable for psychodynamic treatment, much can be learned about every patient if psychodynamic theory is applied in constructing clinical management plans.

Nowadays psychodynamic therapy incorporates the teachings of many writers. Indeed there is today an acknowledged overlap between psychodynamic and other psychotherapies, especially in emphasising the importance of the quality of the therapist–patient relationship. Psychoanalysts undoubtedly use the behavioural techniques of modelling and reinforcement. Conversely cognitive therapists study 'schemas' arising from early life experiences and note misconceptions which psychodynamic therapists call transference projections.

This compartmentalisation of training is understandable in order to promote a rigorous and disciplined guide. In everyday practice, however, the multiple physical, social, psychological and ethical dilemmas facing older people, and their effects on those caring for them, require some plasticity of approach to treatment. Psychodynamic therapy is just one of these approaches.

References

Abraham, K. (1919) 'The applicability of psycho-analytic treatment to patients at an advanced age', in D. Bryan and A. Strachey (eds) *Selected Papers on Psychoanalysis*, London: Karnac.

Balint, M. (1968) *The Basic Fault*, London: Tavistock.

Bowlby, J. (1979) *The Making and Breaking of Affectional Bonds*, London: Tavistock.

Canete, M., Stormont, F. and Ezquerro, A. (2000) 'Group-analytic psychotherapy with the elderly', *British Journal of Psychotherapy*, 17(1): 94–105.

Donovan, S.J. and Roose, S.P. (1995) 'Medication use during psychoanalysis: a survey', *Journal of Clinical Psychiatry*, 56(5): 177–178.

Duffy, M. (1999) *Handbook of Counselling and Psychotherapy with Older Adults*, New York: Wiley.

Erikson, E. (1966) 'Eight ages of man', *International Journal of Psychoanalysis*, 2: 281–300.

Freud, A. (1966) *The Ego and the Mechanisms of Defence*, 1993 edition, London: Karnac.

Freud, S. (1905) 'On psychotherapy', in *Standard Edition*, 1964, Vol. 7.

Gabbard, G.O. (1989) 'Splitting in hospital treatment', *American Journal of Psychiatry*, 146(4): 444–451.

Garner, J. (1999) 'Psychotherapy and old age psychiatry', *Psychiatric Bulletin*, 23: 149–153.

Hildebrand, P. (1986) 'Dynamic psychotherapy with the elderly', in I. Hanley and M. Gilhooly (eds) *Psychological Therapies for the Elderly*, Beckenham: Croom Helm.

ICD-10 (1992) *The ICD-10 Classification of Mental and Behavioural Disorders. Clinical Descriptions and Diagnostic Guidelines*, Geneva: World Health Organisation.

Jaques, E. (1965) 'Death and the mid-life crisis', *International Journal of Psycho-analysis*, 46: 502–514.

Jung, C.G. (1931) 'The stages of life', in H. Read, M. Fordham and G. Adler (eds) *Collected Works*, 1960, Vol. 8, London: Routledge.

King, P. (1974) 'Notes on the psychoanalysis of older patients', *Journal of Analytical Psychology*, 19: 22–37.

King, P. (1980) 'The life cycle as indicated by the nature of the transference in the psychoanalysis of the middle aged and elderly', *International Journal of Psycho-analysis*, 61: 153–160.

Martindale, B. (1989) 'Becoming dependent again: the fears of some elderly patients and their younger therapists', *Psychoanalytic Psychotherapy*, 4: 67–75.

Murphy, S. (2000) 'Provision of psychotherapy services for older people', *Psychiatric Bulletin*, 24: 181–184.

Newton, N.A. and Jacobowitz, J. (1999) 'Transferential and countertransferential processes in therapy with older adults', in M. Duffy (ed.) *Handbook of Counselling and Psychotherapy with Older Adults*, New York: Wiley.

Porter, R. (1997) 'The psychoanalytic psychotherapist and the old age psychiatry team', in R. Jacoby and C. Oppenheimer (eds) *Psychiatry in the Elderly*, 2nd edn, Oxford: Oxford University Press.

Segal, H. (1964) *An Introduction to the Work of Melanie Klein*, London: Heinemann.

Storr, A. (1979) *The Art of Psychotherapy*, London: Secker & Warburg and Heinemann Medical Books.

Tauber, Y. and Van der Hal, E. (1998) 'Countertransference and life-and-death issues in group psychotherapy with child Holocaust survivors', *American Journal of Psychotherapy*, 52(3): 301–312.

Terry, P. (1997) *Counselling the Elderly and their Carers*, London: Macmillan.

Winnicott, D.W. (1958) *Collected Papers*, London: Tavistock.

Yalom, I.D. (1985) *The Theory and Practice of Group Psychotherapy*, 3rd edn, New York: Basic Books.

Zagier Roberts, V. (1994) 'Caring and uncaring in work with the elderly', in A. Obholzer and V. Zagier Roberts (eds) *The Unconscious at Work: Individual and Organisational Stress in the Human Services*, London: Routledge.

Chapter 3

Cognitive behaviour therapy

Philip Wilkinson

Historical background

Cognitive behaviour therapy (CBT) has its early origins in both behaviour therapy, which emerged in the 1950s, and cognitive therapy, which emerged in the 1960s. Behaviour therapists viewed neurotic illness as the product of faulty learning in response to environmental events. This gave rise to new treatment approaches, and great progress was made in the management of the anxiety disorders – for instance, agoraphobia – although attempts at treating depression by reducing reinforcing behaviours were less successful (Rachman 1997). Behaviour therapy did not make specific reference to thoughts (cognitions) but, with the later emergence of cognitive theories, emphasis was given to the importance of faulty cognitive processing in the production of psychiatric problems. In contrast to psychoanalytic theory, the principal area for attention in the emerging cognitive therapy was current conscious thought rather than insight into unconscious processes. A pioneer in the field of cognitive therapy was Albert Ellis, who recognised that distorted thinking in emotional disorder took the form of certain self-commands which were often based on general views in society (Ellis 1962). His approach to modifying these views was one of direct and energetic confrontation.

Another pioneer in the field of cognitive therapy was Aaron T. Beck who also recognised the importance of biased thinking (negative automatic thoughts) and linked this with distorted underlying beliefs about the self and the world. Beck's therapeutic techniques were less confrontative than those of Ellis, relying on an active collaboration between patient and therapist. The earliest application of Beck's cognitive therapy was in the management of depressive illness, and subsequently it has been applied to a range of anxiety disorders, eating disorders and psychosis. Aspects of Beck's model have been validated in older patients, such as the operation of negative automatic thoughts in depression (Lam *et al.* 1987).

Theoretical model

According to Beck's cognitive model of emotional disorders, an individual's mood and behaviour are largely determined by the beliefs she holds about herself and the world (Beck 1976). These beliefs give rise to cognitions or negative automatic thoughts which mediate feelings and influence behaviour. Beliefs are often quite specific to the individual and may only give rise to difficulties in particular circumstances. For instance, older adults who hold the belief that their self-worth depends on their work may only become vulnerable to depression when they face retirement. Further support for this view comes from life events research; examining the beliefs of older patients, Cochran and Hammen (1985) observed that depressed patients typically viewed important life events as entirely out of their control.

As cognitive therapy has developed, the original model has been refined to explain a range of clinical disorders. In depressive illness, for example, patients typically experience biased thoughts regarding themselves, their future or the world around them. Depressed older adults may blame themselves for adverse events, believe things will go wrong again in the future, or hold an over-generalised view of the world as uncaring. Their behaviour will be characterised by withdrawal from pleasurable and productive activities. In anxiety disorders, patients typically experience thoughts predicting danger or catastrophe. In panic disorder, for instance, patients misinterpret physical symptoms of anxiety and predict imminent collapse from a heart attack. In health anxiety, patients are over-vigilant to innocuous physical symptoms and expect to develop serious illness; this may give rise to excessive or inappropriate help-seeking from doctors.

In summary, CBT is based on the view that emotional disorders arise from faulty information processing. Unhelpful biased thoughts underlie problematic emotions and are maintained by the patterns of behaviour that result. Therapy aims to give the patient an understanding of these processes and equip her with techniques to overcome them.

Applications of cognitive behaviour therapy and selection of patients

Assessing a patient for CBT begins with a standard clinical interview to identify problems, previous history of psychological problems and response to any previous psychological therapy. The selection process also involves educating the patient about the nature and format of CBT. The therapist will inform the patient about the skills that may be learned to help with her problems and how these will be tried out between therapy sessions. Patients may, however, require help in specifying their problems and aims (see next section). Those who are curious about the origin and nature of their symptoms are clearly going to be more attracted by therapy, along with those who are motivated to learn a self-help approach. It is often assumed that patients who can easily identify negative thoughts will benefit from CBT. However, the ability to reel off troublesome thoughts (as may be the case with a depressed patient) is not as good a guide as the ability to grasp the wider cognitive model.

Patients receiving cognitive behaviour therapy are often suffering from anxiety problems or depressive illness; therapy of these disorders is described in the next section. As with other psychological treatments, CBT is unlikely to be effective as a sole treatment for severe or psychotic depression, although it can be used to help patients recovering from severe depression. However, CBT is now increasingly being applied in the management of patients with delusions and hallucinations. This work, which has largely been with younger adults, helps patients to reattribute the origin of their psychotic symptoms, identify triggers and correct maintaining factors.

As CBT involves the acquisition of new skills, memory and comprehension are important to its success. This is not to say, however, that patients with mild cognitive impairment cannot benefit from its application. Sensory skills, language and the ability to write are also important in therapy, although adaptations may help to get around these problems (see next section). Although there is little research evidence to help the therapist to identify patients who are likely to respond to CBT, Segal *et al.* (1995) have produced a useful list of criteria (Box 3.1). These criteria apply principally to patients receiving standard short-term therapy (12 to 16 sessions) which is the focus of this chapter. Segal *et al.*'s criteria were derived and

---

Box 3.1 Factors predicting positive response to short-term CBT

The ability to identify and describe automatic thoughts or images, particularly of a self-critical nature.

Patient's understanding is compatible with the cognitive rationale: for instance, patients who insist that their problems are the result of a chemical imbalance are less likely to benefit.

Acceptance of personal responsibility for change.

Alliance potential in the session with the therapist.

Alliance potential out of therapy: evidence of ability to establish intimate relationships and success in previous therapeutic relationships.

Chronicity of problems: short-term problems are more likely to respond to short-term therapy.

Security operations: does the patient employ self-protective strategies such as controlling the interview?

Ability to remain focused.

Ability to differentiate between emotions.

Source: Segal *et al.*, 1995.

---

evaluated with younger adults. It is often observed that older adults need help in sticking to a focus in therapy. The ability to differentiate between emotions may be less applicable to older adults (Shapiro *et al.* 1999).

CBT can also be modified for longer-term use to help people with more complex or entrenched psychological problems such as personality disorder. These approaches take account of the difficulties such patients may have in using conventional cognitive behavioural techniques, and include work on their fixed negative beliefs about themselves (schemas) (Young and Behary 1998). In an attempt to maintain attachment to others, patients with negative schemas may repeatedly engage in unfulfilling patterns of interpersonal behaviour. These, of course, are likely to impact on the alliance with the therapist who will need to employ specific techniques to maintain a therapeutic alliance (Safran and Muran 2000). The reader may observe the similarities between schema-focused CBT and cognitive analytic therapy (see Chapter 6).

The principal focus of this chapter is short-term CBT with individual patients. CBT can, however, also be used with groups of older adults experiencing similar disorders (usually depression or anxiety). Group therapy follows a similar format to individual therapy but often with a greater emphasis on education on the nature of depression and on specific therapy techniques. Time is allowed for each patient to try putting techniques into practice and to feed back homework. Group therapy can have some advantages over individual therapy in that witnessing the work of other group members may help patients to understand the relevance of the cognitive model and engage in treatment.

Therapy in practice

Goal-setting

In a short-term treatment it is important that the best use is made of the time available and that, together, patient and therapist are able to assess its success. For this reason, therapy goals must be set at the start of treatment. Certain self-evident goals such as 'to feel better' or 'to cope with life' must be refined for a number of reasons: first, to encourage the patient to think of what might be realistic and achievable even in the face of significant adversity. For instance, a patient experiencing intermittent pain had given up a number of enjoyable activities, but after discussion of her problems she set a goal of resuming gardening at the times when her pain allowed. Second, in instances such as bereavement or permanent disability where change is not possible, goal-setting may facilitate acceptance and help the patient to find ways of living with their situation. A patient who had lost her husband suddenly was experiencing significant guilt; she set a goal of being able to visit her husband's friends again to talk about his death and enjoy their company. Third, goal-setting can help to reduce a sense of crisis or hopelessness by prioritising problems. A man with multiple physical illnesses and depression was struggling to look after himself and keep in contact with his friends; he also believed he should move to a smaller residence, but felt paralysed by the process of choosing a new home. With help, he set a number of small, achievable short-term goals such as getting up every morning and re-contacting friends. His longer-term goal was to make a decision about his home which, as his mood lifted, he was able to do. Finally, the process of goal-setting may reveal unhelpful thoughts or beliefs which need to be addressed later in therapy. Older patients may, for instance, have exaggerated thoughts, such as 'I'm entirely responsible for myself' or 'Others will not want to help me', which get in the way of recovery. In summary, patients' initial goals may be general and based on feeling better, but further definition of achievable and flexible aims sets the scene for therapy and allows progress to be objectively assessed.

Introducing the patient to therapy

Older patients may be less used than younger people to thinking of themselves or their problems in psychological terms, leaving them daunted by the need to engage actively in a two-way exchange with a therapist. Add to this the range of techniques available in therapy and it is clear that the process of introducing patients to cognitive behaviour therapy will be important to its success. The therapist needs to understand the patient's attitude to therapy from the start; the patient will require a grasp of what the therapy is, and will need to become accustomed to its language and expectations. The language adopted will depend largely on words that the patient is familiar with. One patient, having grasped the concept of negative automatic thoughts, proceeded to call them her 'misinterpretations'. Patients may sometimes choose to use the phrase 'I feel' for thoughts, which is acceptable provided both patient and therapist are able to differentiate between thoughts and moods. Therapy manuals and information sheets read between sessions offer the patient an additional opportunity to grasp the basis of therapy and to understand its relevance to their problems. One widely available manual draws on the example of a man suffering depression in his retirement (Greenberger and Padesky 1995). Introducing the patient to the expectations of therapy involves explaining the importance of the patient's own work between sessions, both in reporting back their observations to the therapist and in trying out different approaches to their problems.

Formulation of problems

Following assessment, the patient and therapist work together to derive a formulation (or conceptualisation), which is a written representation of the patient's problems. This allows the therapist to check that the problems have been correctly understood. The formulation will include the key symptoms that have been elicited, separating them into thoughts, moods, behaviours and physical symptoms. In deriving the formulation, the patient may require help in recognising what is meant by moods and thoughts. Examples of moods can be given and the patient can be asked to describe times when they have felt sad, angry, excited, etc. Sometimes it helps to give the patient a list of possible moods to take away between sessions to use to record how they are feeling at different times. Noticing changes in mood also helps to engage the patient in recognising underlying thought patterns. Questions such as 'what was going through your mind when you began to feel low?' or 'what did that mean to you at the time?' are useful. For example, a depressed patient was quite able to recognise periods of depressed mood, but during mood monitoring she discovered that these were also followed by a sense of anger. This shift in mood alerted her to the thoughts 'I'm inadequate to feel like this . . . I may as well kill myself!' Further clues to thoughts come from unexpected shifts in behaviour or physical sensations. For instance, a carer found himself suddenly shouting at his wife with dementia. Recounting the episode to his therapist he recalled the thought 'she ought to know I'm too busy to help her!' At night he would wake with palpitations and sweating, with the thought 'what if I'm ill, who will take care of her?' It is these immediate, and often idiosyncratic, thoughts that are required for a cognitive behavioural formulation.

A simple diagram can be used to illustrate the formulation. The example in Figure 3.1 was derived with a depressed patient in session one of therapy. Later, as therapy progresses, more information is gathered on relevant aspects of the patient's history. This, together with an understanding of her beliefs, can be incorporated into the type of formulation shown in Figure 3.2.

Once derived, a formulation helps the therapist set the scene for treatment by indicating how changes in one area (such as behaviour or thoughts) may lead to improvement in another (mood). A range of therapeutic techniques is applied to help bring about these changes. This is illustrated in a description of the treatment of depressive illness which is a frequent application of CBT with older adults.

Activity scheduling in depression

Depression is characterised by self-critical thoughts (e.g. 'I'm useless'), thoughts about the world around (e.g. 'I'm on my own') and hopelessness (e.g. 'the future will be lonely; there's nothing I can do

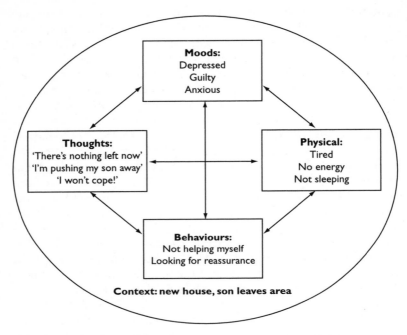

Figure 3.1 Simple formulation of depressed older patient's problems.
Source: based on Padesky and Mooney 1990.

to help myself'). Over-generalised thoughts occur, such as 'I will never enjoy anything' or 'everything I do fails', which lead to loss of motivation and under-activity. The depressed patient, who is often lacking concentration, may find that her thought patterns are very difficult to break into. The cognitive therapist therefore starts by explaining how in depression negative thoughts, low mood and inactivity are linked in a spiral, and then asks the patient to keep a detailed record of her activity on an hourly basis to illustrate this pattern. Simple measures are included of how much she is enjoying activities (pleasure) and how much she believes she is succeeding (mastery). This exercise will illustrate the biased perceptions that occur, particularly a tendency to devalue achievements that have been made or to predict lack of pleasure that may be gained. The record then serves as the basis for modifying activities to increase success, reduce rumination and improve mood. To achieve this, the patient is shown how to plan activities that are realistic and

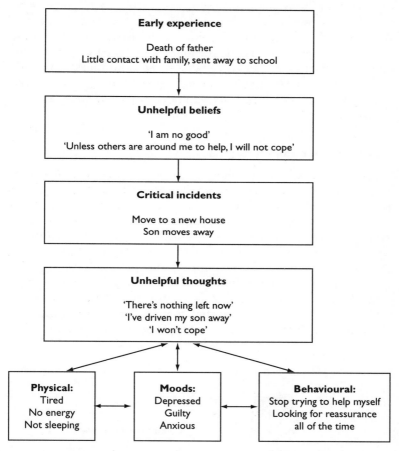

Figure 3.2 Formulation of depressed older patient's problems (same patient as in Figure 3.1). Detailed formulation showing biographical information and beliefs.

Source: based on Fennell 1989.

achievable within her current level of functioning and which may give rise to pleasure or a sense of achievement. This planning should take place in advance so that activities are not dependent on motivation at the time; planning should be specific and on an hourly or half-hourly basis. This process can lead to a rapid improvement in mood as the patient begins to take some control over her depression, and in mild cases of depression these techniques may be sufficient to achieve significant change. Clearly, older patients who are unable to return to their full range of previous activities may also need help in planning suitable alternative activities; the patient's therapy goals may help with this. Older patients may also experience fluctuations in energy due to physical illness, in which case they may need help in discriminating between this and lowered mood, and in adapting their expectations day-to-day according to physical state.

Learning to manage thoughts

Depressed patients often report that their negative thoughts are overwhelming, particularly in the mornings, which blocks effective activity scheduling. In this case it may be helpful to teach methods of distraction, such as switching attention to external objects or focusing on pleasant memories (Fennell 1989). Once mood has lifted and concentration is improved, however, the therapist can begin to use examples of the patient's thoughts to illustrate their biased content. Gallagher-Thompson and Thompson (unpublished) suggest the 'negative headset' of depression as a useful metaphor to illustrate this (Figure 3.3). Targeted questions are also used, such as 'What was going through your mind just before you started to feel

The negative headset helps introduce the patient to the role of biased thinking in depression. When a radio headset is not tuned properly, the listener may mishear or misinterpret the signal from the radio. In depression, the patient's 'personal headset' is tuned to a negative signal which interprets events in a distorted fashion.

Figure 3.3 The negative headset of depression.

Source: CBT therapy manual for older adults (Gallagher-Thompson and Thompson, unpublished).

this way?', 'What does this say about you?', 'What are you afraid might happen?' (Greenberger and Padesky 1995). It is important to write these thoughts down both during and between sessions, both to clarify the content of the thought and also because seeing them written down paves the way for challenging the thoughts. The way in which thoughts are written out may depend on patients' needs. Initially, the therapist will write them out on paper or a white-board. Later they may be entered into a thought diary. The patient is also asked to rate the intensity of her mood at the time and the intensity of her belief in the thought, in a three-column diary (Figure 3.4). To help develop the skill of identifying thoughts she is asked to keep these diaries between sessions for discussion at the subsequent therapy session. In some instances, thoughts may be experienced as images rather than in verbal form. For example, one patient's records showed recurrent images of his deceased sister, associated with depressed and guilty mood; exploration in the next session then revealed his associated verbal thoughts to be 'I didn't do enough for her, she's suffering now.'

Once the patient is familiar with recognising biased thoughts, she is given help to challenge them. This process may already have started, for in the course of verbalising and writing thoughts down, patients frequently recognise distortions themselves. Again, a range of questions can be useful in helping to draw out bias (Box 3.2). An individual patient will usually find one or two particular questions to be most helpful.

Thought challenging is easiest during therapy sessions but, as with thought identification, for the technique to be helpful it needs to be practised between sessions. Successful challenges to thoughts can be recorded in a five-column diary (Figure 3.5). Another approach to modifying unhelpful thoughts is to test them out in a

Situation	Mood	Thoughts
Sitting at home in the morning	*Depressed 80%*	*'I ought to clean the house'* 50% *'I'm useless now'* 90%

In the second column, the patient has recorded the nature of her mood (depressed) and its intensity at the time (80%). In the third column she has identified the thoughts behind her mood, along with their intensity.

Figure 3.4 Three-column thought diary kept by older depressed patient learning to identify biased thoughts.

Box 3.2 Questions to help patients challenge biased thoughts

What is the evidence?
Am I confusing a thought with a fact?
Would this thought be accepted as correct by other people?
Am I jumping to conclusions?

What alternative views are there?
Am I assuming my view of things is the only one possible?
How would I have reacted before I was depressed?

What is the effect of thinking the way I do?
Does this help me or hinder me?
Does it help me to achieve my goals?
Am I asking questions that have no answers?

What thinking errors am I making?
Am I thinking in all-or-nothing terms?
Am I exaggerating how often things go wrong?
Am I blaming myself for something that is not really my fault?
Am I expecting myself to be perfect?
Am I taking personally things that have little to do with me?
Am I paying attention only to the bad side of things?

Source: Fennell 1989 by permission of Oxford University Press.

---

practical way through *behavioural experiments*. For instance, the thought 'nobody will want to talk to me' may lead a depressed patient to withdraw from others, thereby confirming the patient's prediction. In therapy this connection is pointed out to the patient who is then asked to consider what might actually happen if she did in fact start conversations with people. The reality is of course that a proportion are likely to react favourably, and even if others do not, this is not necessarily a reflection of whether the patient is likeable. With this in mind the patient then develops a specific plan for initiating conversations in an appropriate situation, whilst observing what happens, in order to challenge her biased prediction of events.

Work between therapy sessions

Tasks to be carried out between sessions, such as thought challenging or a behavioural experiment, may appear very threatening to older patients who may be keen to succeed or not let the therapist down. The therapist will need to check this out with the patient and

Situation	Mood	Thoughts	Challenge to thoughts	Outcome
Sitting at home in the morning	*Depressed 80%*	*'I ought to clean the house' 50%*	*This is too vague. I can't do the whole house while I'm feeling like this.*	*I will start off with smaller tasks that I can manage.*
		'I'm useless now' 100%	*I'm writing myself off just because I feel depressed. This is all-or-nothing thinking.*	*More helpful thought: 'I'm not functioning as I used to, but there are good reasons for that.'*
				Mood now: depressed 40%

As well as recognising her mood and biased thoughts, the patient is challenging her thoughts by becoming aware of thinking errors. As a result she is able to make more realistic statements to herself (column 5), with a reduction in the intensity of her depressed mood (from 80% to 40%).

Figure 3.5 Five-column thought diary kept by older depressed patient learning to challenge biased thoughts.

suggest solutions if necessary. Some patients may have great difficulty in completing formal diaries, and the therapist must emphasise that the correctness of homework tasks is not important but what is needed is evidence that the patient is able to recognise thoughts as they occur. Some older patients prefer to use short prose accounts of their thoughts rather than tables; others may ask a carer to record them. The author has also had some success using brief telephone contact with patients between sessions to remind them of what the homework is about and to discuss success or problems in carrying it out. If possible, short twice-weekly therapy sessions may be more productive. In summary, what is needed is evidence that the patient is actually putting the techniques into practice in day-to-day settings in order to achieve change.

Learning to manage beliefs

According to the cognitive model, a patient's biased negative thoughts are underpinned by certain beliefs or *rules for living*. These usually reflect long-held views to do with the patient's culture and developmental experiences. Many beliefs we hold are balanced and adaptive and serve us well in life, such as 'To stay well I must eat well.' Other beliefs, however, are unhelpful because they have the same absolute or all-or-nothing quality of unhelpful thoughts, such as 'I am unlovable.' Interestingly, the beliefs which predispose to problems in older patients have often been useful over many years until they come to encounter new situations in later life. For example, one man with the belief 'If I work at it, I can manage any situation' had led a satisfying and productive life running a business; he even avoided becoming depressed following a stroke by working tirelessly at his rehabilitation. However, when his wife died in front of him after a short illness he experienced recurring images of her death, blamed himself and thought there must have been a warning sign of her imminent death which he failed to detect. As beliefs emerge, the therapist may point them out to the patient for inclusion in the formulation. Later in therapy, after the patient is familiar with managing unhelpful thoughts, work on beliefs can help to prevent recurrence of depression in the future. A range of approaches can be applied, such as looking for the origins of beliefs and examining advantages and disadvantages. Beliefs will only change slowly as the patient practises at not always living in accordance with these rules and recognizing when they are active.

On a cautionary note, because older patients may have lived most of their lives according to certain rules, challenging them in therapy may be threatening. During therapy, one patient's mood dipped considerably when she recognised how her belief 'I'm inadequate' had led her to withdraw from people and opportunities for most of her life. However, examination of an older patient's core beliefs can also provide a fruitful opportunity for life review. Identifying the origins of beliefs and the influences upon them requires the patient to recount key biographical information. Within a cognitive framework this can help the older patient to re-appraise the meaning they have attributed to stages in their lives. For instance, a former refugee identified the belief 'If I am to succeed, I must put my home country behind me.' Although he had coped well for many years, he recognised that this belief was fuelling his depression in later life and that he now needed to integrate his early experience into his current life. It is the author's observation that this can prove a potent therapeutic tool, especially for patients with reduced cognitive functioning who may have difficulty manipulating thoughts.

Treating anxiety

The interventions described so far apply to the treatment of patients with depressive illness. Another frequent application of CBT is in the management of anxiety disorders such as generalised anxiety, panic, or social phobia. From a cognitive perspective, anxiety arises when situations are interpreted as threatening. Catastrophic predictions give rise to anxiety symptoms and the sufferer may resort to a range of behaviours such as avoidance, escape or other actions to try to avert catastrophe, such as holding on to objects to prevent collapse. For instance, in the cognitive model of panic (Clark and Ehlers 1993), bodily sensations such as innocuous chest pains or anxiety symptoms are interpreted as signs of imminent collapse, leading to a sudden upsurge in anxiety (see Case illustration 1, p. 63). In older people, panic attacks may be triggered by the symptoms of cardiorespiratory illness. People suffering with social phobia fear that others will judge them negatively. They appraise social situations as dangerous, fearing rejection by others, and so stay away from such situations or pay excessive attention to how they might appear (Wells 1997). In older adults this may occur when events cause people to have to enter new situations or when they suffer physical changes such as facial weakness or hemiparesis following stroke. In generalised anxiety disorder, people often have a fear of not coping in the future and experience excessive worry which becomes a threat in itself. Recently, a cognitive behavioural treatment for post-traumatic stress disorder (PTSD) has been developed (Ehlers and Clark 2000). A PTSD sufferer re-experiences her trauma through intrusive thoughts or images as if the trauma is presenting a current threat. Treatment may be applied to older patients who have experienced single traumas such as accidents or traumatic bereavements. There is also increasing interest in the treatment of chronic or delayed-onset PTSD – for instance, following wartime experiences.

The general principles of cognitive behavioural treatment of anxiety problems include introducing the patient to the cognitive model of her disorder and modification of anxiogenic cognitions by thought-challenging techniques and modification of avoidance and safety behaviours. These techniques can also be adapted to treat anxiety in patients with mild memory loss in dementia (Koder 1998). To achieve this, information on anxiety is simplified and supplemented by written material, while thoughts are challenged using behavioural experiments rather than more abstract written methods. It may also be possible for an appropriately-informed carer to sit in on sessions to support work between sessions. It is unclear at present whether these approaches should be accompanied by memory training, as this might reinforce the exaggerated importance a patient already places on being able to remember (Kipling *et al.* 1999).

CBT for patients facing real-life problems

It is frequently asked how cognitive therapy can help people facing real-life problems. It is true that CBT involves challenging unrealistic thoughts, whereas people experiencing situations such as life-threatening illness may of course report understandable pessimistic and anxious thoughts. Recent developments, however, show that there are a number of ways in which CBT may be helpful. Careful problem identification and appropriate goals are important first steps so that therapy can focus on helping the patient to cope with the secondary effects of their problems. One patient who identified his main problems as severe irreversible chest disease and having just entered a nursing home could not see that therapy could possibly help. He was then asked to list the problems that arose from his situation, and he identified loss of contact with his son, loss of pleasurable activities because of tiredness, and fear of not being able to breathe. These then set the scene for a successful course of therapy. Many of the advances in working with people facing adverse life circumstances have been made with patients suffering with cancer (Moorey 1996). This work highlights the importance of facilitating emotional expression in the normal process of adjustment, rather than applying CBT at all stages. Patients who make a poor adjustment or become depressed, however, may benefit from cognitive techniques such as distraction from overwhelming thoughts or exploration of the underlying personal significance of events. A number of practical approaches may help, such as using activity scheduling to regain even a small amount of personal control over the situation, or planning for the future of one's family. The following extract from Moorey's work illustrates the use of activity scheduling and a behavioural experiment with a physically ill patient.

> A patient with carcinoid syndrome had spent 15 years fighting recurrences of the disease with numerous operations. Each time he made a rapid recovery and returned to his old self as soon as possible. When he took longer over his recovery from his most recent operation he became initially frustrated and then depressed. He thought that if he could not be cheerful and cope without any help from others he was useless. He believed his family would be better off without him because he was useless and a burden to them. The therapist encouraged the patient to engage in some small activities that could be helpful to his family and at the same time asked him to test his belief by asking them if they did indeed feel they would be better off if he were dead. The response was a very moving, open display of affection from his grown-up children that they had not been able to show before. This convinced him that he was valued and needed and led to marked improvement in his mood.
>
> (Moorey 1996, pp. 466–467)

An important group of elderly people facing adverse circumstances are the carers of dementia sufferers. This group is prone to developing depression, particularly if they have a past history of depression and are caring for someone with marked behavioural and psychiatric symptoms of dementia. They frequently experience guilt, frustration, hopelessness and a loss of control over their lives. Cognitive behavioural techniques can be successfully combined with education on the nature of dementia in order to relieve carer burden (Marriott *et al.* 2000). A carer's unhelpful thoughts are often misunderstandings of certain of the dementia sufferer's behaviours, particularly lack of motivation, sequencing problems, soiling or emotional disturbance (James 1999); frustration or anger arises when these are interpreted by the carer as deliberate malevolent acts (Gallagher-Thompson *et al.* 1992).

Specific cognitive approaches may be helpful with older patients facing regret at the end of their lives. If a patient has regret over a decision made earlier in her life she is asked to review the circumstances in which the decision was made, as she may be overlooking other people and factors involved in the decision at the time and judging herself unfairly from her current perspective. Although a bad choice was made, actually having made a choice at the time may not have been a bad thing. Patients may also selectively attend to things that appear to have gone wrong. For instance, if the outcome years later had been favourable, would the patient still be attributing so much personal responsibility? If the regret is over a decision made more recently (for example, moving to a smaller house), after which the patient has become depressed, is the patient using her depression as evidence of a faulty decision? If so, she may be helped by learning that depressive reactions are common after such changes, but that this does not invalidate her reasons for moving. Instead, she is encouraged to actively tackle her depression using the techniques learned in therapy.

In working with older adults it may also be necessary to address a patient's predictions regarding her death and what she will leave behind. What are the effects of her thinking? Is she preoccupied with the apparent unfairness of her life and is this preventing her from taking some control over the rest of her life? Is it helpful to be considering the period immediately following her death instead of, for instance, thinking a hundred years ahead (Carlson 1997)? This might help a patient to gain some perspective over the consequences of her death or help her to gain a balanced view of her life as a whole, not just its later stages.

The following case examples illustrate the application of CBT with patients experiencing panic disorder and late-life depression.

Case illustration 1: a man with panic disorder occurring on retirement from work

Mr Balfour was a 65-year-old man who was referred for psychological help by his general practitioner because of sudden attacks of fear, dizziness, chest tightness and tingling fingers. These had started after he was asked to begin making plans for retirement from his job as a glazier. He came from a family with a strong history of heart disease and had lost his father during childhood. As a child he himself had been ill with a heart infection, and it was said he might die. He was married and had had a successful working life. A perfectionist by nature and prone to worry he enjoyed good physical health, but was under review by his general practitioner for borderline high blood pressure although he showed no signs of heart disease.

He admitted worrying about the prospect of his retirement, particularly how he would fill his time and support his family. He had a high score (28) on the Beck Anxiety Inventory (Beck *et al.* 1988), but his Beck Depression Inventory score was low at 7 (Beck *et al.* 1961). It was agreed at the outset of treatment that the initial goal would be to help him to learn ways of managing his panics, though accepting that he might not achieve full resolution of his symptoms. A secondary goal was to enable him to approach his retirement with greater confidence.

Mr Balfour's problems were conceptualised at two levels: first, the current pattern of thoughts and behaviours maintaining his symptoms, and second, the background to his problems and the circumstances responsible for triggering them. The current pattern of symptom maintenance was described with reference to a cognitive model of panic (Clark 1986). He had begun to realise that attacks often came when he was tense, hungry or angry, and could occur almost anywhere. They seemed to be triggered by physical symptoms such as feeling hot or dizzy in busy shops. This indicated to him that he might be about to faint and risk hurting himself, or even be about to die from a heart attack. The resulting upsurge in fear led to additional physical symptoms of racing heart, chest tightness, abdominal churning and tingling in the fingers. These symptoms in turn provided additional evidence of a heart attack. This formulation was represented diagrammatically (Figure 3.6). Assessment also revealed that certain behaviours were perpetuating his symptoms and thoughts. For instance, whenever he felt dizzy or

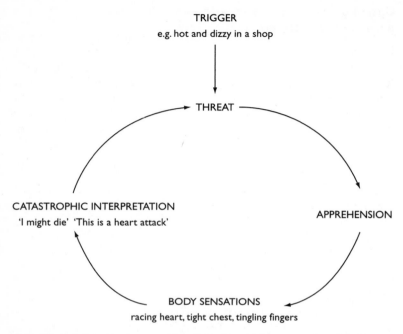

Figure 3.6 Relationship between Mr Balfour's thinking, mood and behaviour during panic attacks.

Source: based on Clark's model of panic disorder (Clark 1986).

noticed his heart racing he would sit or lie down or at least grip on to a nearby object. This, he said, prevented him from fainting and prevented further strain on his heart. Preferably, however, he would avoid reaching such a state by leaving or avoiding situations which brought on symptoms, such as crowded shops. Throughout the day, and especially when he thought he was at risk, he would scan his body for symptoms or monitor his heart rate. He recounted his first attack when, on a hot day, he had driven his wife to an open market and arrived hot and anxious. Almost immediately, he noticed that his heart was racing and that his chest was tight. Fearing that a heart attack was imminent he took refuge in the car and controlled his breathing, believing that he had averted disaster for the time being. These factors were summarised in the fuller formulation shown in Figure 3.7.

The guiding principle of treatment was to enable Mr Balfour to

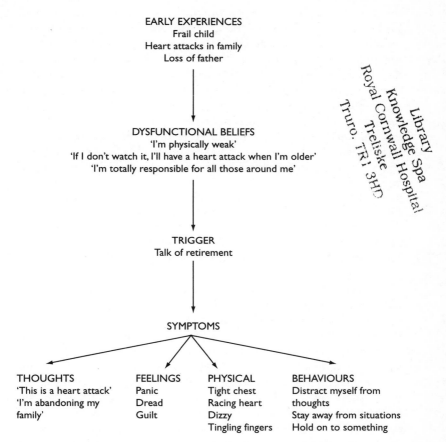

EARLY EXPERIENCES
Frail child
Heart attacks in family
Loss of father

DYSFUNCTIONAL BELIEFS
'I'm physically weak'
'If I don't watch it, I'll have a heart attack when I'm older'
'I'm totally responsible for all those around me'

TRIGGER
Talk of retirement

SYMPTOMS

THOUGHTS	FEELINGS	PHYSICAL	BEHAVIOURS
'This is a heart attack'	Panic	Tight chest	Distract myself from
'I'm abandoning my	Dread	Racing heart	thoughts
family'	Guilt	Dizzy	Stay away from situations
		Tingling fingers	Hold on to something

Figure 3.7 Formulation of background and precipitants to Mr Balfour's problems.

change his interpretations of physical symptoms to a realistic, non-catastrophic understanding. This was achieved through helping him to observe and understand his thought patterns, then challenging them through a combination of reviewing evidence, abandoning safety behaviours and facing feared situations. The total of six treatment sessions are summarised.

In session one, the formulation was agreed with Mr Balfour. He recognised that 'some of the symptoms I feel, like dizziness, are affected by the way I think', and in order to help him recognise the link more easily he agreed to keep a record of episodes of panic and the thoughts he was having before the next session. In session two, his homework was reviewed and revealed many examples of catastrophic thinking, including having a head-on collision whilst driving and leaving his wife alone not knowing how to cope in life. He had spontaneously tried out controlling a panic by concentrating hard on something else, with a little success, but with help he recognised that this coping strategy was unlikely to help him in the longer term as it would not reduce his belief that his anxiety symptoms were harmful. It became evident that he held a belief that sooner or later he was destined to have a heart attack. He based this on being physically weak in childhood and having his many relatives dying of heart attacks. The background threat of imminent retirement activated his belief that he was solely responsible for those around him, which he likened to his attitude as a child after his father's death. With this new understanding, Mr Balfour's symptoms had already reduced considerably. He agreed to go on recording thoughts and situations, and to review his formulation before the next session.

In session three, Mr Balfour reported some success in averting a panic attack before giving a retirement speech at work, by recognising his anxiety symptoms for what they were and not interpreting them in a catastrophic fashion. In the session, a behavioural experiment was carried out in which he was asked to breathe whilst keeping his lungs over-inflated. He was warned that this would induce a feeling of breathlessness, which to him predicted that he might succumb to a heart attack. The exercise did induce breathlessness, chest wall tightness and some tingling in the fingers. He continued for over ten minutes, confirming to him that some of his symptoms were induced by normal physiological mechanisms and were not evidence of impending collapse. On the basis of this, he suggested commencing a few regular press-ups to remind him of this at home, and he agreed to continue keeping thought records.

By session four, Mr Balfour had learned that chest pain does not indicate an imminent heart attack. He discussed an episode in a shopping centre when he controlled a panic attack by escaping to a coffee bar, trying not to think about his anxiety. He suggested more helpful responses, including learning to answer thoughts back and to stay in the situation. For homework he agreed to visit a city centre shop on a Saturday afternoon to try thought challenging. In the next session, he reported successfully visiting a shop, although he was not always able to challenge his negative thoughts, so was still resorting to distraction. His history of hypertension was discussed, revealing that he believed his blood pressure soared to life-threatening levels each time he became anxious. The evidence for this was reviewed and in homework he agreed to record and challenge negative thoughts relating to his blood pressure, to work out his strategies for the future. By session six, he had made good use of his alternative attitudes to his blood pressure, as shown in his thought diary (Figure 3.8).

At the end of therapy, Mr Balfour had experienced a significant reduction in the frequency and intensity of his panic attacks. He planned to continue to practise facing feared situations and challenging unhelpful thoughts to support this. He had greater confidence planning his retirement and recognized the specific importance of continuing physical activity both to maintain health and to remind him that physical symptoms can be innocuous. He kept a record of useful techniques in his therapy workbook.

Case illustration 2: a lady with physical problems and depressive illness

Mrs Jacobs was a 78-year-old lady referred for therapy by her general practitioner having developed a depressive illness following a stroke. She had been treated by him with a course of antidepressants, which had brought about a small improvement although she remained significantly depressed and anxious with a 'dread of the future'. She described a loss of confidence and poor concentration and had withdrawn from a number of social activities. She had also noticed a deterioration in her memory, finding it difficult to retain and use new information, although this did improve at times when her mood picked up. Of note in her earlier life Mrs Jacobs had been married and had three grown-up children who did not live locally. She had studied at university and had enjoyed a career as a teacher until retiring at the age of 63 years. She had coped with a number of stressful events in her past, such as wartime events and the loss of her husband, without becoming depressed. Her medical history included hypertension, heart disease and arthritis. Her stroke had occurred after her return from holiday, giving rise to permanent weakness of her right leg causing her to walk more slowly. Evaluation by a neurologist, including magnetic resonance imaging, had confirmed the presence of cerebrovascular disease. Fearing further strokes, she became anxious that she would not be able to carry on

Situation	Emotion	Unhelpful thought	Evidence that it's true	Evidence that it's not true	Alternative thoughts	Emotion
Saturday – shopping in town	Fear 80%	'I'm going to have a heart attack'	Feeling flushed: head pounding	This is just anxiety: it's happened many times before	'It doesn't matter if I get anxious' 'It's not a heart attack' 'My blood pressure does not shoot up'	Fear 10%

This is an alternative form of thought diary to the five-column diary shown in Figure 3.5. In this diary, the patient is helped by columns 4 and 5 to evaluate the evidence for a thought before coming up with an alternative thought.

Figure 3.8 Mr Balfour's thought diary: challenging biased thought associated with panic attacks.

with her interests which included committee work and trips to the theatre. She feared that she would be unable to continue living independently and would have to move to a nursing home to avoid becoming a burden to others. She lay awake thinking about these problems but her mind was 'a fog' and she was unable to manage any effective problem-solving. Her therapy goals, which reflected these problems, included being able to manage social and business events and being able to plan realistically for her future.

In session one Mrs Jacobs began to recognise the patterns of thoughts and behaviours which were taking place in her depression. She realised that she had become very conscious of the change in her walking which resulted from her weak leg, thinking that other people were noticing it and commenting on it. This added to her anxiety and caused her to avoid social situations or instead to go to lengths to check that people were not likely to reject her because of it. These observations were included in a simple formulation (Figure 3.9) and this set the scene for her to keep a simple diary of these

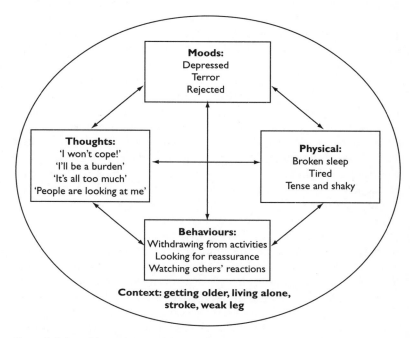

Figure 3.9 Initial formulation of Mrs Jacobs's depression.

Source: based on Padesky and Mooney 1990.

thoughts and behaviours as they occurred at a committee meeting before session two. She immediately recognised the biased nature of these thoughts, which brought about some improvement in her mood. In session two Mrs Jacobs was helped to notice the link between her mood, energy and activity. At times she was quite tired, with her mind 'in a fog', which caused difficulty in organising activities such as catching up on tasks at home. This led to self-critical thoughts such as blaming herself for not being able to get enough done or for not enjoying things. She expected herself to function as she had before her stroke, discounting any achievements she was now able to make. She was also disappointed by the day-to-day fluctuations in her energy which occurred as a consequence of her age and physical state. To illustrate this process she kept a diary between sessions. She was given written information about the link between activity and depression, and before session five was asked to begin activity scheduling. This caused her some difficulty as she aimed to complete the activity schedule perfectly, bringing to attention the high standards she had always set for herself. The exercise also brought to the therapist's attention the extent to which Mrs Jacobs was struggling with mental tasks because of her cognitive slowing. Mrs Jacobs was encouraged to plan things in advance but to allow some flexibility depending on her physical state and external events. She approached larger commitments by breaking them into smaller stages and using more written records. To support these changes she successfully challenged her self-critical thoughts with responses such as 'The list of jobs will never finish, so why blame myself?', 'Is it really important to do it now?' The beliefs underlying Mrs Jacobs's high standards were examined – for example, the belief that 'I must always do everything to the best of my ability' – and she began to accept that getting older allowed her the opportunity to relax her standards and take some rest.

In session six, Mrs Jacobs was helped to use thought challenging to deal with her fear of rejection by friends. She found that questions such as 'What am I afraid might happen?' and 'Am I exaggerating the importance of events?' were particularly useful. She learned to test out some of her predictions using simple behavioural experiments. She recognised a tendency to predict that people would not want her and so had become very vigilant to signs of perceived rejection. If others were ambiguous in their behaviour (such as not initiating conversation) it was taken as evidence that they did not want her around. She tested out her thoughts using simple behavioural experiments such as initiating conversation with people and being ready to challenge unhelpful thoughts as they arose. She found that actually putting this into practice was not always easy, so she needed to plan the stages in some detail beforehand, then complete her thought records and observations soon afterwards. She was successful in reducing the intensity of her thought that she was being rejected from 80 per cent to 5 per cent.

By session nine, Mrs Jacobs was becoming more able to be flexible in her day-to-day activities and was coping better with personal relationships. She was still feeling anxious and low in the mornings, when she tended to wake early feeling anxious and despondent. She had hopeless thoughts and although she could challenge these thoughts successfully later in the morning, she had difficulty doing this at the time. She therefore developed a list of strategies to cope with depression in the morning, such as keeping a reminder by her bed of the challenges to unhelpful thoughts and activities she could engage in rather than lying in bed ruminating.

By session ten Mrs Jacobs's mood was significantly improved. She still reported mild cognitive deficits such as difficulty naming and slower thinking, presumably related to her cerebrovascular disease. She identified unhelpful thoughts about developing Alzheimer's disease or losing control of her life. With the therapist she also identified a distortion in her thinking that having irreversible problems (such as her vascular disease) meant she had an unmanageable problem. Understanding the physical basis to some of her problems also helped her to challenge her self-critical thoughts. At times of additional stress, such as admission to hospital, she would become anxious and depressed and her fears for the future would recur, but she managed to use thought challenging to handle this (Figure 3.10). This also helped her to review the plans she had made in case of further disability in the future, such as financial planning and adding her name to the list for her preferred nursing home. At the end of treatment, Mrs Jacobs made a therapy 'blueprint' which included a summary of what she had done to achieve her improvement and what she would need to do if her problems recurred (Box 3.3).

Summary

Cognitive behaviour therapy is an active, focused psychological treatment with an increasing range of applications. It can be used to

Situation	Emotion	Unhelpful thought	Evidence that it's true	Evidence that it's not 100% true	More balanced thought	Feeling now
Planning admission to hospital	Anxiety 60%	'I shan't be able to manage'	My children are too busy to help	If they're busy, they still haven't forgotten me	'It's OK to seek out help'	Anxiety 5%
	Depressed 80%	'I might have to ask for help'	I'm having to make all the arrangements	My neighbour did offer to help	'This is how I feel when I'm under pressure'	Depressed 10%
		'I'm all alone'	People won't ask how I'm getting on	If they don't ask, it doesn't mean they don't care	'Yes, I'm in charge of my life. It's hard work, but it doesn't mean I'm alone in the world'	

Figure 3.10 Mrs Jacobs's seven-column thought diary.

> *Box 3.3* Extract from Mrs Jacobs's therapy blueprint giving advice to herself on what to do to prevent or manage future problems
>
> 1 Prioritise my time and don't be too hard on myself if I don't get things done.
>
> 2 Watch out for times when I predict the future. Just try to take things as they come.
>
> 3 Remember that having to sort things out for myself doesn't mean I am alone in the world.
>
> 4 Be aware of future setbacks, e.g. illness, practical problems.
>
> 5 If the problems recur do the following:
>   * refer to therapy notebook
>   * re-read my information on strokes and vascular disease
>   * keep thought records
>   * if necessary, seek refresher session with therapist

---

treat mild to moderate depression and may improve the longer-term outcome if used as an adjunct to antidepressant medication (see Chapter 7). Therapy is based on a shared formulation of clinical problems which incorporates patients' physical as well as psychological symptoms. Therapy involves a range of therapeutic techniques, many of which can be used successfully with older adults.

Further reading for patients

Greenberger, D. and Padesky, C.A. (1995) *Mind Over Mood: Change How You Feel by Changing the Way You Think*, New York: Guilford Press.

References

Beck, A.T. (1976) *Cognitive Therapy and the Emotional Disorders*, New York: International Universities Press.

Beck, A.T., Ward, C.H., Mendelson, M., Mock, J. and Erbaugh, J. (1961) 'An inventory for measuring depression', *Archives of General Psychiatry* 4: 561–571.

Beck, A.T., Epstein, N., Brown, G. and Steer, R.A. (1988) 'An inventory for measuring clinical anxiety: psychometric properties', *Journal of Consulting and Clinical Psychology* 56: 893–897.

Carlson, R. (1997) *Don't Sweat the Small Stuff . . . and It's All Small Stuff:*

Simple Ways to Keep the Little Things from Taking Over Your Life, New York: Hyperion.

Clark, D.M. (1986) 'A cognitive approach to panic', *Behaviour Research and Therapy* 24: 461–470.

Clark, D.M. and Ehlers, A. (1993) 'An overview of the cognitive theory and treatment of panic disorder', *Applied and Preventive Psychology* 2: 131–139.

Cochran, S. and Hammen, C. (1985) 'Perceptions of stressful life events and depression: a test of attributional models', *Journal of Personality and Social Psychology* 48: 1562–1571.

Ehlers, A. and Clark, D.M. (2000) 'A cognitive model of posttraumatic stress disorder', *Behavioural Research and Therapy* 38: 319–345.

Ellis, A. (1962) *Reason and Emotion in Psychotherapy*, New York: Lyle Stuart.

Fennell, M.J.V. (1989) 'Depression', in K. Hawton, P.M. Salkovskis, J. Kirk and D.M. Clark (eds) *Cognitive Behaviour Therapy for Psychiatric Problems: A Practical Guide*, Oxford: Oxford University Press.

Gallagher-Thompson, D. and Thompson, L. (unpublished) 'Patient therapy manual for depressed older adults', Stanford University.

Gallagher-Thompson, D., Rose, J., Florsheim, M., Jacome, P., DelMaestro, S., Peters, L., Gantz, F., Arguello, D., Johnson, C., Moorehead, R.S., Polich, T.M., Chesney, M. and Thompson, L.W. (1992) 'Controlling your frustration: a class for caregivers', Palo Alto Health Care System.

Greenberger, D. and Padesky, C.A. (1995) *Mind Over Mood: Change How You Feel by Changing the Way You Think*, New York: Guilford Press.

James, I.A. (1999) 'Using a cognitive rationale to conceptualize anxiety in people with dementia', *Behavioural and Cognitive Psychotherapy* 27: 345–351.

Kipling, T., Bailey, M. and Charlesworth, G. (1999) 'The feasibility of a cognitive behavioural therapy group for men with mild/moderate cognitive impairment', *Behavioural and Cognitive Psychotherapy* 27: 189–193.

Koder, D. (1998) 'Treatment of anxiety in the cognitively-impaired elderly: can cognitive-behavior therapy help?', *International Psychogeriatrics* 10(2): 173–182.

Lam, D.H., Brewin, C.R., Woods, R.T. and Bebbington, P.E. (1987) 'Cognition and social adversity in the depressed elderly', *Journal of Abnormal Psychology* 96: 23–26.

Marriott, A., Donaldson, C., Tarrier, N. and Burns, A. (2000) 'Effectiveness of cognitive-behavioural family intervention in reducing the burden of care in carers of patients with Alzheimer's disease', *British Journal of Psychiatry* 176: 557–562.

Moorey, S. (1996) 'When bad things happen to rational people: cognitive therapy in adverse life circumstances', in P.M. Salkovskis (ed.) *Frontiers of Cognitive Therapy*, New York: Guilford Press.

Padesky, C.A. and Mooney, K.A. (1990) 'Clinical tip: presenting the cognitive model to clients', *International Cognitive Therapy Newsletter* 6: 13–14.

Rachman, S. (1997) 'The evolution of cognitive behaviour therapy', in D.M. Clark and C.G. Fairburn (eds) *Science and Practice of Cognitive Behaviour Therapy*, Oxford: Oxford University Press.

Safran, J.D. and Muran, J.C. (2000) 'Resolving therapeutic alliance ruptures: diversity and integration', *Journal of Clinical Psychology* 56, 233–243.

Segal, Z.D., Swallow, S.R., Bizzini, L. and Rouget, B.W. (1995) 'How we assess for short-term cognitive behaviour therapy', in C. Mace (ed.) *The Art and Science of Assessment in Psychotherapy*, London: Routledge.

Shapiro, A.M., Roberts, J.E. and Beck, J.G. (1999) 'Differentiating symptoms of anxiety and depression in older adults: distinct cognitive and affective profiles?', *Cognitive Therapy and Research* 23: 53–74.

Wells, A. (1997) *Cognitive Therapy of Anxiety Disorders: A Practice Manual and Conceptual Guide*, Chichester: Wiley.

Young, J. and Behary, W.T. (1998) 'Schema-focussed therapy for personality disorder', in N. Tarrier, A. Wells and G. Haddock (eds) *Treating Complex Cases: The Cognitive Behavioural Approach*, Chichester: Wiley.

Chapter 4

Systemic therapy

Jane Pearce

A system is defined as 'a set of things connected, associated, or interdependent, so as to form a complex unity' (*Oxford English Dictionary*). Systemic therapy recognizes the connections and interdependencies between members of a system, and the role they play in the resolution of the problems that one of its members is experiencing. The family is a significant context for people with mental health problems and has been the system most commonly addressed in theory and practice of therapy. In older age, a number of people beyond close family are also significant and involved in a person's daily well-being. For the most vulnerable, daily life is lived with the support of a network of carers, friends and professionals, or in a care home. This chapter will look at therapeutic approaches that might promote healthier functioning for older people and those connected with their lives.

Historical background

The roots of family therapy can be seen in the social work movement of the late nineteenth century. Attempts were made to assist whole families, often with their basic needs for housing and food, rather than focus on the individual with a psychological problem. Secondly, the child guidance movement developed clinics to offer counselling for the parents and teachers as well as the child presenting with difficulties. Developing psychoanalytical theory, and Freud in particular, had postulated that the early interactions of the child with its mother were the origin of later psychological problems.

The focus of treatment remained on the individual until the work of John Bowlby marked a shift towards the inclusion of the family (Bowlby 1949). Psychodynamic theory developed with the recognition and description of groups as more than a collection of individuals (Bion 1948). Psychodrama groups (in which vignettes from daily life were enacted) could be seen as a transitional step towards viewing families as small groups (Moreno 1945). Also of particular relevance was the research into the significance of family functioning (particularly communication) for schizophrenia (Bateson *et al.* 1956).

While research interest in psychiatry shifted to biological treatment methods, a number of schools of family therapy developed with a common interest in the interpersonal processes within family groups. Family therapists developed theoretical constructs of the processes operating in the families that they worked with, and developed a range of diverse ideas about treatment. Ackerman (1958) pioneered the application of psychodynamic therapy with families. The aim was to give insight into the interpersonal methods that individuals used (unwittingly) to manage their unconscious impulses and conflicts, but which were interfering with the family's ability to function effectively or to adapt when necessary. Minuchin (1974) described a structure of appropriate and healthy relationships among family members. The resulting structural family therapy approach aimed to disrupt unhelpful coalitions or inappropriate alliances (such as over-involvement or 'enmeshment' between generations) or to clarify age-appropriate generational boundaries.

Development of systemic approaches in old age psychiatry

The potential for family interaction to influence problems and adaptation to ageing was recognized some time before family therapy was first applied in this age group (Spark and Brody 1970). A problem-focused brief therapy model was the earliest application of family therapy to age-related issues (Herr and Weakland 1979). This established the precedent of working with adults in the context of their families and caring agencies, including residential homes and hospitals. In parallel, however, different therapeutic interest in the older generations was growing with the suggestion that emotional illness in a family member might have its origin in the difficulty that previous family members experienced separating from the core family (Bowen 1978). The older generation should therefore be seen in therapy in order to trace the patterns down the generations. Interest emerged later in understanding the balance of family obligations and debts transmitted across the generations and across the lifespan of multigenerational relationships (Boszormenyi-Nagy and Spark 1984). The 'family ledger' (or balance of obligations and debts) could be settled in a later generation.

Subsequently, a number of different types of family therapy have been applied successfully to older people and their support systems or families (Pottle 1984, Hargrave and Anderson 1992, Richardson *et al.* 1994, Qualls 1995, Gilleard 1996, Asen 1997). No unitary model has evolved.

Theoretical model

All models of family therapy are systemic in nature in that they utilize a conceptual framework that recognizes the interconnectedness of the individual, family and social phenomena. The presented problem is to be examined within the interpersonal context of the family or caring network, rather than within the intrapersonal context. The patient becomes the 'presented' or 'index' patient and is seen along with others who are important in their current context. Thus, rather than looking at dad's depression, it will be the experience of dad's depression for each person that is explored.

The systemic therapy model acknowledges that family members influence and are influenced by one another. An underlying concept is that the whole is greater than the sum of the parts (Bertalanffy 1968). A family is more than just the composite individuals and its properties and characteristics could not be predicted only from information about each of the individual members. The quantity and quality of information released during a systemic consultation is therefore different from that obtained when the individual members are seen separately. Moreover, it is possible to observe actual interactions between family members rather than merely to obtain reports of them. Behaviour and presentation may be very different in the presence of significant others.

The processes between the members are shaped by cycles of ongoing communication through behaviour, expectations and beliefs about behaviour and reactions to behaviour. These can be seen as **circular processes** in which it is hard to distinguish the causal and consequential events since the consequences of one event may be causal for another. This is illustrated in Figure 4.1 using a common pattern in later-life depressive illness. Where a number of

A *Father* depressed, lets things slip at home, has not paid bills.

B *Son* starts to do more for father, takes over the bills and sees the house needs repairs.

C *Father* finds he needs so much help, if only his son could come more often.

A *Father* feels a burden, helpless; he cannot cope and experiences depression.

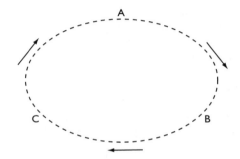

Figure 4.1 Circular process.

people are involved, it may be arbitrary to distinguish a cause and consequential event at a particular point in time since this will depend upon the point at which a sequence of interactions is examined.

Healthy functioning of a family is characterized by both stability and the capacity to change. Each family will have its habitual patterns; familiarity and predictability both confer the sense of knowing how and upon whom to depend or trust, and enhance the ability for the individual to plan for his or herself. Some patterns are *de facto* dysfunctional and have never served a useful function. However, even a pattern that works at one stage in life may become redundant. A capacity for change is required when circumstances change, and a new pattern of organization is needed in order to continue to maintain reliability and predictability. For example, the father may have always made the decisions but may become indecisive following a stroke; yet the family may still wait for him to make decisions. Symptoms emerging around the time of such a change in fitness or capability may be seen from the systemic point of view as serving a homeostatic function, and preventing change (for example, perhaps by delaying potential changes for other members).

Stability and change will be seen operating as a family moves through its lifespan. Both predictable and unpredictable events will challenge a family as it moves through time from birth to death (Carter and McGoldrick 1989). The change that an individual experiences may make changes necessary in some of their relationships, hence trigger the need and provide the opportunity for change in other members. Where these are 'in phase' (e.g. the death of an older parent), they may be easier to cope with than when the events are 'out of phase', such as the death of a teenager or grown child.

The ways in which transitions have been negotiated at earlier developmental stages in the lifespan will be the backdrop for the later-life transitions (Walsh 1989). The progress made with separation and individuation during adolescence may have resulted in limited autonomy or some degree of enmeshment between family members. This may have been relatively stable during mid-life, masked by geographical distancing or emotional detachment. However, as dependency of the older person emerges, conflicts and anxieties can be unmasked. Age-related demands may also bring family members into enforced proximity or face-to-face with emotion, especially when possible death, or enduring dependency, is presenting. Responses may not fit the current circumstances, and emotions belonging to a prior developmental stage may surface. For example, the old sibling rivalries can re-emerge. Long-standing disappointment may be reawakened in a grown son or daughter who has not resolved their feelings about their parent who never lived up to their childhood ideals.

There are a number of reasons why family or systemic interventions are applicable in work with older people. Families remain an active, purposeful and powerful interpersonal context for the majority of older people. Even in the absence of close physical contact, there can still be 'intimacy at a distance'; purpose and meaning can be maintained through memories, phone calls and photographs as well as through visits (Spark and Brody 1970). The family roles taken by older people include care of grandchildren and assistance in times of crisis (such as divorce or illness). It is generally only in the very last years of life that older people become dependent. Older people are active in meeting social and emotional needs, and they are vulnerable to ripple effects of events within their families such as divorce and remarriage. Physical sequelae of ageing and associated illnesses certainly raise the potential thought of reliance on others and can bring the threat of, or reality of, changes in autonomy. These in turn can challenge the generational roles. They can also bring a number of possible agencies and services, as well as grown children, siblings, friends and neighbours, into regular contact with older people's lives.

Applications of systemic therapy and selection of patients

Systemic ideas can be incorporated into everyday practice in assessing problems and comprehending families. Individual components of assessment technique and simple intervention can sit alongside standard assessment and treatment methods. Family therapy can be combined with a broad range of interventions including drug therapy and other psychological treatment methods. A single systemic family meeting may be all that is needed in order to mobilize a family that has good resources to call upon.

Pragmatically a key criterion for selection of patients for systemic therapy is the interest and willingness of relevant members of their family or network. For some patients it can be a relief when members of the family are invited to meet together. For others the referrer plays a much more important role in facilitating the acceptability of a systemic intervention. The referrer may be helped in their effectiveness at this stage by clarifying some key areas in their decision to consider referring. These are summarized as a series of questions in Box 4.1.

The referrer may be clear as to who is connected to the problem or its resolution and the roles they play. Many older people live within a very small nuclear family, alone or with one other family member. However, a number of people beyond close family may be involved in, or be significant for, their daily well-being; these may include a neighbour or carer or a relative with daily phone contact. While families are the common focus of the primary social unit, when an older person is living in a residential setting the social unit may include key staff as well as the relevant members of the family, or the staff alone. There will often be reason to consider the

---

Box 4.1 Selection of patients: questions for the referrer

What is the main problem to be solved?

Who is most concerned that it is addressed now?

Who else is involved in the problem?

Who is likely to be essential at a family meeting if this therapy option can go ahead?

What is the best way to convey information on:

- Purpose and effectiveness of family meetings?
- What to expect during a family meeting?

Would written information be helpful?

---

involvement of members of both systems (Smyer *et al.* 1988). The person who wanted the referral, and the patient, can be asked who is significant.

Willingness of at least some of the key people identified may be sufficient to recommend systemic therapy. Identified system members will then need introductory explanation as to why a meeting is to be offered. It is crucial that they have an idea of how this might help, above and beyond the liaison they have already perhaps experienced with a number of other professionals. They also need realistic expectations of how the family team will work, so that they feel prepared for a new approach. The potential for people to feel coerced should be actively considered, because of both the ethical importance and the negative impact on efficacy of therapy. The key points are summarized in Box 4.2.

Situations and problems that might benefit from family assessment and interventions are summarized in Box 4.3. Illness and disability

---

Box 4.2 Information to be given to families in advance of first systemic meeting

---

Why family meetings are offered (family problems are common; it helps to get together)

Practical conduct of a family session

Purpose and activity of a team if there will be one

Provisions for consent and choice for use of video if used for supervision

Confidentiality

Box 4.3 Possible applications of systemic approaches

Dependence
Over-dependence on others
Under-dependence and rejection of help
Conflict of opinion
Decisions on moving into residential or nursing-home care

Illness-related difficulties
Prolonged psychological illness such as depression and dementia
Psychosocial problems with severe or chronic physical illness (e.g. stroke, chronic airways disease)

Care-giving
Carer support
Conflict of needs
Abuse

---

can become embedded in circular processes, and challenge family members to make transitions in their roles and relationships (see 'Theoretical Model', pp. 78–79). Patterns of behaviour and interaction intended to help solve difficulty may create other problems (Herr and Weakland 1979). Systemic therapy could address these processes. Systemic interventions can also enhance support for the primary care-giver (Fisher and Lieberman 1994), or increase compliance with or efficacy of other treatments – for example, physical rehabilitation for communication difficulties post-stroke (Burns 1996). Family crises may arise over decisions about moves into long-term care. These can be hard to tackle because of guilt and other emotions. Family conflict may arise when moves are seen to be precipitate or premature. New stressors emerge following placements, including interaction with staff and staff attitudes, feelings of loss of control and powerlessness to control care (Zarit and Whitlatch 1992, Bonnel 1996). Systemic work with care staff from the long-term care home together with the patient's family members may be helpful.

In situations of elder abuse, family interventions may be a means to engage abusive families who are otherwise unable to utilize support and practical help (Richardson *et al.* 1994). The question here may be 'How does the older person's dependence fit into the whole family system?' Psycho-educational interventions for families may have the aim of preventing abuse of relatives after discharge from medical or psychiatric in-patient settings (Banks *et al.* 1986).

Because family therapy involves discussion amongst a number of people, the sensory skills of hearing and seeing are both important. Extra consideration should be given to avoiding noise both within and outside the room. Air-conditioning or echoey rooms can create a problem even with minimal impairment of hearing. When a participant appears to be missing visual or spoken cues at times, this may reflect part of the family communication pattern; however, there may be a remediable practical explanation. The work involved in finding an effective way of fully including the individual with sensory impairments may be therapeutic in its own right. Creative ways of ensuring that patients with reduced visual and hearing skills are not disadvantaged can be agreed within the meeting; for example, it may be useful to have explicit cues for whose turn it is, naming the person you are talking to, and, if need be, who is speaking.

Memory, comprehension, and concentration skills are also important. When skills are even minimally impaired, sessions may need to go at a slower pace, be shortened or include use of frequent summary statements. Written notes of feedback or tasks can be used. It is quite possible to include someone with cognitive impairment in family meetings in a therapeutically positive way (Jeffery 1987, Benbow *et al.* 1993). Relatively few differences in technique are needed when a member of a family meeting has dementia. It is suggested that the content of 'emotional memory' is more enduring than cognitive function (Hargrave and Anderson 1992). It is also suggested that the process of turn-taking in discussion is more meaningful than the verbal content (Roper-Hall 1994). A person with dementia may benefit from being there and being taken seriously, even if not remembering what was said.

Therapy in practice

The description used here is of an eclectic, systems-based model. A range of family interventions has been found effective, but there is no research base on which to recommend a specific approach in work with older people. Elements from different types of family therapy have been successfully combined and applied together for older patients (Pottle 1984, Benbow *et al.* 1993, Roper-Hall 1994, Shields *et al.* 1995). The therapeutic tool is the meeting with the therapist, who uses a process of assessment to understand the structure and function of the presented problem within the family and, if necessary, uses interventions to mobilize the system in a way that results in change. The meeting should offer a neutral forum with a structure in which to share time both to talk and to listen. Given the heterogeneity of problems that might be addressed through systemic therapy there is no general advice on number of sessions. Following the first meeting, a recommendation can be given on whether further assessment or an intervention would be helpful. Single assessment consultations can be effective, but an intervention may require several sessions before symptoms change. See Box 4.4.

The family therapist ideally works as part of a small team with other colleagues of varying professional backgrounds including nursing, psychology, medical, or social work. The whole team will discuss the referral but, during the therapy session, usually just one team member will act as the therapist in the room with the family. The team may observe from an adjacent room supported by aids such as a one-way screen, and a microphone, telephones and earpiece to communicate during the session. Therapists can offer to introduce their colleagues face-to-face at the end of the session; there is no secrecy as to their identity, but, to avoid complication and distraction from what is happening within the family they are not in the room. The team assists in maintaining the focus within sessions and will discuss face-to-face with the therapist during breaks in the sessions. Their observations amplify the information

---

Box 4.4 Stages in therapy

1 Bringing together members of the system
Planning a meeting
- Who is to be invited to a meeting?
- Developing hypotheses about the problem

2 Systemic assessment meeting
Engagement of system members
Understanding the presenting problem
General assessment of the system

3 Planning for interventions
Developing a collaborative partnership between therapist and system members
Exploration to find out how ready the system is for change
Identifying and sharing expectations for improvement

collected during a session, and they can help the therapist to reach an understanding of what is going on, and give their suggestions on how best to assist the family in tackling the problems.

Lone working can be successfully used if sessions are adapted to include clear plans for breaks out of the room during the session to collect thoughts and make notes for later, as well as making video and audio recordings which can be used to supplement discussion in supervision.

Bringing together members of systems

Before the family is seen, ideas or initial hypotheses about what might be going on in relation to the problem are developed and decisions made on whom to invite. See Box 4.1 (p. 82) The minimum for an effective systems or family meeting is likely to be: the person viewed as the patient, those known to be most concerned about the problem, and anyone who would be a key supporter or carer for the patient. There may be apparently key people who cannot see that there is a problem. Here flexibility and willingness to work with those who agree to come together in the first instance can still prove helpful. If it emerges that those absent occupy a position that prevents change, then more effort may be necessary in order to facilitate their involvement, even if only for a once-off attendance.

When practical reasons preclude travel, home-based and outreach therapy may be effective, despite the therapist having to work alone or with colleagues sitting in the same room as the family. Relatives are more likely to live at a distance than is the case with younger patients, and there may be practical problems in getting relatives to attend meetings. Imaginative ways of including those who are not geographically close, or for whom illness prevents attendance, include sending tapes of the session, written messages and specific requests for views and comment (Gilleard 1996). These steps may *per se* open up new routes of communication.

The assessment stage commences with engagement of the family through clarification of the background to the referral and expectations of the meeting. This helps everyone to be on the same footing and will be important as a basis on which to develop a therapeutic alliance. Information on the practical aspects should be given verbally at the start of the first systemic session and consent established (refer back to Box 4.2, p. 82). Doubts and reservations about therapy may be expressed during engagement, for a number of reasons. First, if the older person suffers from an organic disorder such as dementia or a serious physical illness, there may be an expectation that something should be done to the patient to solve the problem. To the family the older person may either be or have been the problem.

Secondly, where there are issues of dependence raised in the presenting problem, it is likely that feelings of guilt, blame or failure will also be present to a greater or lesser extent. These may be with regard to the patient or between family members. They may inhibit members' willingness to come together unless there is an understanding that the meeting can be an opportunity to clarify the effects of a problem, to pool resources for coping with it, or perhaps to explore new ways of coping. The therapist may simply want to ask the family to meet in order to help them in their work with the older person.

Thirdly, many of the themes surrounding the illnesses or problems of older 'index patients' may be anxiety-provoking for other family members since they frequently raise thoughts of loss of capacity and death. Doubts about talking in front of the 'patient' can arise particularly in the presence of dementia. It is reasonable to say that this is best sensitively evaluated within the family meeting. The wish to maintain secrets about fears concerning the presence of dementia and loss of capacity can be likened to walking on thin ice. The 'partial secret' influences communication and it may cause more distress if those you love and trust cannot cope with the 'truth'. A patient experiencing evening hallucinations with a mild early dementia said of his family's distress and reluctance to talk with him about their plans for residential care that he knew 'the sword of Damocles' hung over him.

Understanding of the patterns surrounding the presenting problem using a systemic perspective

The initial focus is most usually on the precise effects of a presented problem. These individual effects may be very different for different family members. Each person is asked about what they see as the problem and its effects, and further information may be elicited using circular questioning (this will be discussed below). Views may be sought on opinions as to causes and what should be done. It can take some time to come to any agreement as to what is the most pressing problem and what actually needs to be tackled. Solutions or adaptations tried so far can be explored. Both credit and respect for attempted solutions (even if flawed) should be made explicit.

Exploration of the presenting problem, and further enquiry, can provide the opportunity to find out about the family's communication patterns and relationships and structure. Who tells problems to, listens to and talks to whom, and who not? Are there dyads or triads of communication? How direct is communication, or does it go through one person? Behaviour sequences that control communication may also be seen, such as one person blocking another by interruption or dismissing what the other has said. Is there a tendency to talk for another? Such patterns can easily be dismissed as part of a disability. The power structure of the family may be evident from the interaction patterns – for example, which members of the family make things happen or stop things happening in the family? Frequently power is vested in a coalition. This may be between the generations, such as the parent/child or grandparent/grandchild. It may be that an important powerhouse for the family is not functioning at the current time and that this role is vacant. The family structure can be characterized by the current roles adopted by members and how well these are adjusted to current circumstances; are there boundaries between and within the generations, such as (over-)involvement or disengagement with each other? It can also be characterized by the way in which emotion is expressed and recognized.

Planning for interventions

As the assessment stage is completed, the working understanding, or formulation, of the problem is used to help the family make changes. There are two main considerations: the therapeutic alliance, and family resources and readiness for change.

A key characteristic of successful work with a family is a collaborative partnership (Treacher 1995). The therapist has to be open to each member of the family in order to maintain a position of positive interaction free of expectation and judgement of the family's experience, goals and norms. It is assumed that everything makes sense for this family. They are the experts on themselves, while the therapist is an expert on families in a general sense, and knows about why problems evolve and persist. A spirit of questioning everything can be created such that the therapist can respectfully explore from a slightly different perspective. It is important to strike a balance between collecting information in the assessment and getting in tune with the family. The therapist also has to remain neutral in order to be able to observe the possible alliances between the family members, sub-groups or indeed with the patient. It is easy to pick up a family's views on what is difficult and become aligned with this. It is also possible to form alliances with or against any members of the family or the other agencies currently in contact with or involved in the care of the older person. Transference is not commonly worked on within sessions, although it may be looked at within the team and supervision. Resistance to engagement or alliance may first be looked at in a practical way – have we invited the right people? Do we need to see them at home? Is more support needed before this system can really contemplate the problem?

Secondly, success in giving feedback in a way that families find helpful is linked to how in tune the therapist is with the current resources and readiness for change within the family system. A subsequent recommendation on intervention needs to be a good enough match with where the family is at; for example, are they just at the point of recognizing a problem, or already thinking about the situation differently? How great a degree of system mobility or manoeuvrability does the family have at that point in time (Roper-Hall 1994)? Will natural curiosity now trigger the propensity to change, or is the system awaiting direction? Will it actually resist change? Defining the problem may in fact enable the family to do the rest of the work, especially if they had functioned well up to that point. It may be the first time that the problem has been defined at all for many members who have simply felt anxious and swept along as things that had 'always been' gradually became turned upside down. Crucial information may not have been widely available, or certain key family members' views may not have been heard.

However, the process of defining the precise problem for each person may have revealed that there are competing demands on family members' time, emotions and energy; that the presented problem was covering other problems; or that the adaptations so far tried served a role in ameliorating some other important issues. Indeed there may be conflict of best interests. Further work with the family may be needed. Expectations and objectives for improvement need to be shared. What would be needed in order to make a difference? How would you know when you got there?

Termination of therapy can be discussed once change has started to occur. Discussion of the future can include recognition of progress so far, future strategies to use, and what, if any, ongoing contact there should be with the therapist. It may be agreed to reconvene at a point in the future to review progress, or it may be helpful to offer an open appointment for the family to book if they choose at a future time.

Using techniques and interventions from systemic therapies

This section elaborates on techniques used in the assessment stages and describes a number of potentially helpful interventions which have been successfully used with families of older index patients (Richardson *et al.* 1994, Qualls 1995, Gilleard 1996, Asen 1997). These are summarized in Box 4.5.

A **hypothesis** represents a possible explanation connecting the relevant behaviour of family members in a meaningful manner (Palazzoli *et al.* 1980). Knowledge of common issues, themes and events of later-life families can be combined with ideas from the variety of family therapies to form the basis of one or more hypotheses which may be used to guide exploration of the current problem. As information is gathered in relation to the structure and function of the

---

Box 4.5 Techniques and interventions found useful in practice with systems of older patients

Related to beliefs
Hypothesis formation
Circular questioning
Positive connotation
Paradoxical intervention

Related to context
Genogram
Life review

Related to behaviour patterns
Reframing
Tasks/rituals
Communication skills
Problem-solving skills

presented problem, the hypothesis will be modified and revised. Consider the vignette:

> Mr Smith presented at the age of 86 with a one-year history of symptoms of anxiety and depression. These had become worse despite treatment with antidepressants. He had on occasions contacted the emergency services because of frightening palpitations. Something more needed to be done to treat his illness. He had been registered blind a year and a half previously and had been widowed some ten years before moving to live in an annexe in his daughter's house. The referrer had identified the daughter's distress and felt particularly concerned for Mr Smith's granddaughter who was considering delaying going to college to help her mother out.

Initial hypotheses were based on ideas about the current context (with simultaneous transitions of a daughter divorcing, her own daughter leaving, and a grandfather needing to adapt his role and lifestyle) and about patterns of behaviour (vicious circles of reassurance and monitoring).

Circular questioning was used in the assessment. In circular questioning, questions are not addressed directly to the person concerned. Instead, family members are asked to comment in turn on the thoughts and behaviours of, or relationships between, other members of the family. So, for example: 'Who is most affected – your grandfather or your mother?' 'Which of them is least concerned that your grandfather panics and calls the ambulance?' Questions might focus on behaviour, as in this case: 'What does your mother do after your grandfather has an attack? What does your mother do next, then what does grandfather do next?' Questions could also focus on relationships and changes in relationships, for example: 'Your daughter and granddaughter are very close to each other – did they get close to each other before the divorce or after?' Circular questioning might prompt people to stop and think, attract the interest of those who were not listening, and reduce stereotyped responses. The new information may illuminate differences of opinion or perception of problems. In this particular case, we learned that they had in fact become close in the last year since grandfather had lost his vision.

Hypothetical questioning is another way round concrete answers and can release new information. The past or future can be explored in imaginary situations. 'Supposing your grandfather beats his depression and stops panicking, what will your mum do with her time?' Differences of opinion can be revealed. Mind-reading questions may explore awareness of one another's thoughts and feelings. It could have been used in this example to ask 'If grandmother were alive and here today, what would her opinion be?' Guessing the views of absent family members may reveal differences in relationships or prevalent family beliefs that underlie expectations and roles.

Maps of the structure and function of the patient's system can be drawn. A family **genogram** can be constructed, starting with those involved in therapy, and adding on anyone affected by or helping with the problem. It can be used as a part of assessment to explore previous generations and record the personal family history, its members and events. It can also provide an account of its members' management of and adjustment to problems and progression through earlier family life stages. Roles, relationship patterns, ties and bonds can be explored and drawn in. It can serve as a summary of the information known about the family, a map of family resources, the strengths and vulnerabilities. In Figure 4.2, Mr Clarke (Sebastian) had been abusing alcohol, and was neglectful of self and house. His daughter's family was exasperated that despite their doing so much to encourage his self-care he did not make any effort. His son, Jacob, after many years' estrangement from his father, had made contact and felt he should help his sister sort things out. He had wanted to come to the family assessment. At the stage of drawing the genogram, the role of Dora, Mr Clarke's wife who had died two years before, was emerging. She had been very close to her daughter and the three grandchildren. She had also maintained contact with her son. The genogram started them on the path to telling their earlier life story and paved the way for positive concern about one another.

An **ecomap** can help in understanding patterns and the importance of the broader context of the person's life. This drawing maps relationships beyond the family and includes friends, clubs, voluntary work, post-retirement work contacts, neighbours, church, social services, and health services. Close ties, stresses, frequency of contacts and significant events can be drawn on.

Guided life review is a shared process of looking back at experiences, choices and conflicts (Hargrave and Anderson 1992). Family members add details, broaden and develop understandings and

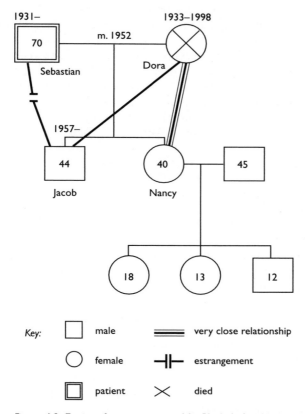

Figure 4.2 Extract from genogram, Mr Clarke's family.

clarify relationships. This can provide an opportunity to assess the remaining resources and conflicts, at this life stage, and to consider the planning of reunions and potential matters for resolution as death approaches. There can be joint work on a summary statement about the older person's life, describing its essential elements or character. Life review may be helpful in increasing emotional bonds and may make it possible to attribute new meanings to past events. This could help to increase empathy where the attachments between the family members have been negative or have not been mutually healthy.

Coaching and rehearsing behaviours, communication, or problem-solving skills can be practised explicitly in sessions – for example, 'Let's have that conversation now' (Zarit and Edwards 1996). It can also be implicit through modelling of the way the therapist talks with the family.

A hierarchical model for assessing the scope for interventions with families of older people is suggested (Shields *et al.* 1995). Problem-solving can work well if family communication is working. If the problem-solving is temporarily overwhelmed, as in a crisis, it may be that support, pointing in the direction of services, giving information and perhaps assisting in problem-solving, is applicable. If communication was based on sound underlying attachments, interventions to structure communication or learning of communication skills may help. If attachments are negative or dysfunctional then these interventions should be prefaced by work to improve empathy and mutual understanding.

Reframing is central to most family therapy interventions (Herr and Weakland 1979). It intends to change the emotional or conceptual setting of an experience or situation. It suggests another setting which could equally well fit the facts of the situation. The new suggestion is not so much the provision of new 'facts' but the introduction of the possibility that alternative meanings for interactions and behaviours can exist; its purpose is to start to change the meaning that an individual attaches to certain behaviours. Typically, it will emphasize the potentially positive aspects of behaviour which up to that point may have been viewed in a negative light. It is often couched in terms of the family's own expressions and phrases, to make it understandable. **Tasks** may be given to be carried out between sessions. These may take many forms, including monitoring (for example, of symptoms or behaviours), instructions to have conversations, rituals to carry out and activities. The purpose is to alter repeated behavioural and interactional patterns closely connected with symptoms.

In the case described above, Mr Smith, his daughter and granddaughter spent much of their time together in discussion of father's symptoms and difficulties. The context of panic and anxiety was reframed in terms of mutual caring and loyalty. Mr Smith had taken a much-valued past active role in the care of his two grandchildren, and his granddaughter was 'willing to make great sacrifices for your grandfather'. A task was suggested to try out alternative behaviour. Mr Smith was to experiment with having two days a week on which he would not say anything about his symptoms, and the two women were to make observations. One month later, at the next appointment, Mr Smith and his granddaughter were more worried about mother, who was anguishing about her lack of confidence about returning to work. Mr Smith had largely discontinued discussing his physical ailments since he found he felt more dignified and reassured that he could cope better through controlling how and when he talked of his woes.

A positive connotation can bring out the positive intentions behind the presenting problem, in a way that indicates how they might be serving the common good (Palazzoli *et al.* 1980). It assumes that people do what they think is best or what they think will prevent something worse. This can open the way for **paradoxical interventions**, in which maintenance of problems is recommended rather than their removal. The intervention is not fanciful because it is based on a plausible explanation of why things are the way they are and the benefits the status quo offers. The advice to restrain from change until a later stage when a different solution is found can be a logical step. It brings the hint of some future that is possibly different and preferable. This intervention may be helpful when patterns of behaviour are very entrenched and are not modifiable by logical means. Mr Clarke's family (Figure 4.2 above) was eventually helped following the positive connotation of his neglect of the house; the team recommended that he should, for the time being, continue to neglect his house as this encouraged everyone to keep in contact.

Case illustration

The case illustration here is of a family intervention, by a team working with an eclectic systems-based model in the management of a resistant depressive illness. The intervention will be described in some detail in order to illustrate the types of issues that emerge, and the responses of the therapeutic team.

Mr White's first episode of agitated depressive illness had started four years previously. He was then 67 years old and presented following an impulsive self-harm episode. This incident closely followed recurrence of a benign condition for which surgery had been required previously. He initially responded to in-patient treatment with antidepressants. His recovery was short-lived and symptoms of low energy, lack of interest and poor concentration had recurred only a few months after discharge. He remained anxious and was reluctant to let his wife out of his sight, fearing she might die. This

prompted referral to community services. A variety of pharmaco-
logical strategies and nursing interventions (including behavioural
approaches to structure activity) were tried. He had not been able to
use anxiety management techniques.

In-patient treatment was offered for electro-convulsive therapy.
Mr White made a partial recovery, but continued to experience
anxiety about his wife's well-being, worrying about her visits to
hospital and making frequent phone calls home to check that she
was well. Four months into the admission, his community psychiatric nurse recommended that the in-patient team should consider a
family intervention because of the impact of Mr White's patterns of
behaviour during periods of leave at home. These were unchanged
from before his admission. On visits home he would lie down on the
sofa from where he would be anxious to keep his wife under his eye,
and tell her what she could and could not do. His two daughters
visited him in hospital and took turns to bring their mother daily to
visit. They were both invited along with their parents to the first
session. One therapist talked in the room with the family. A team
observing through a one-way screen with a microphone supported
her. A telephone between team and therapist was used for any questions, comment or advice during sessions. Before the session, they
agreed to take a break after about forty minutes to discuss and then
offer the family a message.

The hypotheses initially focused on two areas: first the changes in
roles that had followed from the transitions of illness and retirement (common themes for later-life families); second, the structure
of the family since the transitions, in which the women had strong
alliances, with Mr White less actively included.

The first session

Meeting with Mr White, Mrs White and their two adult daughters.
Discussion took place as to the nature of the problem from each
person's perspective. Enquiry was made as to in what way and how
much the problem was affecting each of them. Mr White's view was
that the main problem was that he could no longer look after his
family 'as he should' and that his wife was left having to do everything. There was agreement on the latter point but not without
some sympathy for how difficult it must be for dad, although they
all felt that Mrs White was the most affected of them all. Mr
White's illness, unresolved depression and loss of independence

following his inability to drive were talked about. Views on what he and life would be like when he was well were sought. How would they know if he was better? What would he do or say? Mr White said little at all, even when specifically asked. His replies were short.

The team felt they saw evidence of a caring family and a willingness to work at helping things get better. A message was given to the family reflecting appreciation of the hard work they had been doing battling with these difficulties, and indicating that more would need to be learned about them before any advice could be given. A further appointment was offered.

Second session

Enquiry was made about any observations of change or any events since the last meeting. This was followed by exploration of family membership: the structure and organization of the generation above; how they had been organized and how they had functioned in the middle part of their family life; and how they had been organized since the illness. Mr White had been the boss, and they still described him as such. The team gradually drew the family tree. Mr White had lost his mother young and had been raised by paternal aunts. He grew up to work with them in the family business, subsequently taking this over. Mrs White was from a large family, deriving support from a close relationship with her sister.

The team felt that the current arrangement of strong women reflected Mr White's earlier life experiences and that both hypotheses were still supported by the information so far. The team gave a message to draw attention to the transition to retirement and changes in physical health, and to check out how prepared for change members felt. They told the family: 'You all show you care in different ways. At this time in your life, Mr and Mrs White, there are changes. Some are happening already; there are more to come. Changes are threatening for you, more so for some than others.'

Third session

Feedback on how things were going was requested. Mr White felt that he had changed a bit for the better but would like to be doing more. The others saw little change. Hypothetical questions were used and the family were asked to read the future. 'What would life be like in the next five years if the problem stayed the same, if it got better and if it worsened?' Staying the same might be tolerable for Mrs White if she had more space to get on, it might be acceptable to Mr White, but it would cause continued distress for both the daughters and upset their children. The problem getting better might offer things that they had not had all through life together, such as taking a cruise – much deserved as they had never taken holidays because of work. The possibility of the problem getting worse was seen as potentially catastrophic; Mrs White might either vegetate or at worst lose her health and die.

The team noted the considerable separation anxiety surrounding the behaviours and set a task. The message was that 'The team has heard about the great stress and if there is to be no change you, Mrs White, will need a little rest as a safeguard. To safeguard, you [Mrs White] should ask to take a rest twice a day and to go on the couch. Everyone else should observe how things go.'

Before session four Mr White was discharged home from in-patient care and he attended a local day hospital for after-care.

Fourth session

Observations were sought on the task set in the previous session. Mrs White had taken some rests on the sofa, but because Mr White went and sat in her armchair it was possible to play dominoes, so she had done that. Mr White had noticed the change of having his family around him more and had watched some television. His daughters saw their father as more relaxed, and noted that he had started taking seconds of pudding. They also observed that their parents had been going out to relatives for tea and to play cards.

The team felt that things had moved in leaps and bounds but that the session had got a bit stuck, with a sense of the family becoming disengaged from the discussions. A message was offered to reflect this and contain the change. The team said they were pleased to hear of positive changes, and advised to hold steady. 'Take things no slower or no faster.' They should continue to make observations on changes in any member of the family.

Fifth session

Observations were again requested. Little change was thought to have occurred in Mr White and any improvement was attributed to the day hospital he was attending since he enjoyed some of the practical activities there. Mrs White had, however, been out shopping and he had risen to go out walking looking for her. He had recruited one of his daughters in support of his need to find out where she was. A considerable amount of energy had been expended on anxiety and subsequent guilt. Circular questioning comparing behaviour in the marriage at two different points in time was used. Ten years previously was compared to now. It had always been the case that Mrs White was not to go out while Mr White was at home; only when he was out would she use the opportunity. In the past he would initiate joint outings but not so in the last few years. Discussion of a possible task of further trips out for Mrs White alone clarified that none of them would tolerate 'the uproar' that would follow. The only safe way was to go out during her husband's day hospital attendance.

The team reflected on the containment of anxiety by the current status quo. A reframing was used along with a further task. The message given was that Mr White had been doing a very good job preventing anxiety, panic and guilt by staying put on the sofa, and that Mrs White was doing a good job by knowing the limits, and keeping the peace. They were invited to now be a little more adventurous. Instead of Mrs White being afraid to ask, they should plan as a couple to go out together.

Sixth session

Feedback was invited on the homework. For the first time in a session Mr White had been outspoken and took the lead to report that they had taken a shopping trip out of town by bus, as a couple, without help. The day hospital had reduced attendance because of his general improvement. Only he could see any progress since the previous session. He was described by one of his daughters as no different from when he came out of hospital, and she feared he would end up in hospital again. They agreed that improvement was a long way off and suggested he was just 'putting an act on' for others. He could not do that at home and they saw no change there. The team was interested in the way that the family was regulating itself, and the way in which brakes on Mr White's improvement were being applied.

The team was truly very pleased with how well the homework had been done and that it had been achieved without the help, or knowledge, of the daughters. They said this in a message, and went on to tell Mr White's daughters that there was so much improvement that their parents were well enough to work as a couple. Mr and Mrs White were addressed directly and asked to make a trip to the garden centre and prepare for spring. They would be seen alone next time. They were indeed seen alone and couple work went on to explore the impact of changing roles, now a retired couple, and the adjustment to this.

Summary

Systemic therapy is applicable to later-life problems, and the skills of the family therapist complement generic professional skills used in work with older people. The majority of system contacts occur outside of formal therapy within the natural groups that form around older people. Access to consultancy discussion with experienced teams may enhance the understanding of families.

References

Ackerman, N.W. (1958) *The Psychodynamics of Family Life*, New York: Basic Books.

Asen, E.K. (1997) 'Family therapy with ageing families', in R. Jacoby and C. Oppenheimer (eds) *Psychiatry in the Elderly*, Oxford: Oxford University Press.

Banks, M.E., Ackerman, R.J. and Clark, E.O. (1986) 'Elderly women in family therapy', *Women & Therapy*, 5: 107–116.

Bateson, D., Jackson, D.D., Haley, J. and Weakland, J. (1956) 'Towards a theory of schizophrenia', *Behavioural Science*, 1: 251–264.

Benbow, S.M., Marriott, A., Morley, M. and Walsh, S. (1993) 'Family therapy and dementia: review and clinical experience', *International Journal of Geriatric Psychiatry*, 8: 717–725.

Bertalanffy, L. (1968) *General Systems Theory*, New York: Braziller.

Bion, W.R. (1948) 'Experience in groups', *Human Relations*, 1: 314–329.

Bonnel, B.W. (1996) 'Not gone and not forgiven: a spouse's experience of late-stage Alzheimer's disease', *Journal of Psychosocial Nursing*, 34: 23–27.

Boszormenyi-Nagy, I. and Spark, G.M. (1984) *Invisible Loyalties*, New York: Brunner/Mazel.

Bowen, M. (1978) *Family Therapy in Clinical Practice*, New York: Jason Aronson.

Bowlby, J. (1949) 'The study and reduction of group tensions in the family', *Human Relations*, 2: 123–128.

Burns, M.S. (1996) 'Use of the family to facilitate communicative changes in adults with neurological impairments', *Seminars in Speech and Language*, 17: 115–121.

Carter, B. and McGoldrick, M. (1989) *The Family Life Cycle: A Framework for Family Therapy*, Boston: Allyn & Bacon.

Cohen, P.M. (1983) 'A group approach for working with families of the elderly', *The Gerontologist*, 23: 248–250.

Fisher, L. and Lieberman, M.A. (1994) 'Alzheimer's disease: the impact of the family on spouses, offspring and inlaws', *Family Process*, 33: 305–325.

Gilleard, C. (1996) 'Family therapy with older clients', in R.T. Woods (ed.) *Handbook of the Clinical Psychology of Ageing*, London: Wiley.

Hargrave, T.D. and Anderson, W.T. (1992) *Finishing Well: Aging and Reparation in the Intergenerational Family*, New York: Brunner/Mazel.

Herr, J.J. and Weakland, J.H. (1979) *Counseling Elders and their Families: Practical Techniques for Applied Gerontology*, New York: Springer.

Jeffery, D. (1987) 'Should you involve an older person about whom there is an issue of cognitive competence in a family meeting?', *Newsletter* of Psychologist Special Interest Group working with older people, 24: 8–11.

Minuchin, S. (1974) *Families and Family Therapy*, Cambridge, Mass.: Harvard University Press.

Moreno, J.L. (1945) *Psychodrama*, New York: Beacon House.

Palazzoli, M.S., Cecchin, L., Prata, G. and Boscolo, L. (1980) 'Hypothesizing-circularity-neutrality: three guidelines for the conductor of the session', *Family Process*, 19: 3–12.

Pottle, S. (1984) 'Developing a network-orientated service for elderly people and their carers', in A. Treacher and J. Carpenter (eds) *Using Family Therapy*, Bristol: Blackwell.

Qualls, S.H. (1995) 'Clinical interventions with later-life families', in R. Blieszner and V.H. Bedford (eds) *Handbook of Ageing and the Family*, Westport, Conn.: Greenwood Press.

Richardson, C.A., Gilleard, C., Lieberman, S. and Peeler, R. (1994) 'Working with older adults and their families – a review', *Journal of Family Therapy*, 16: 225–241.

Roper-Hall, A. (1994) 'Developing family therapy services with older adults', in A. Treacher and J. Carpenter (eds) *Using Family Therapy in the 90s*, Oxford: Blackwell.

Shields, C.G., King, D.A. and Wynn, L.C. (1995) 'Interventions with later life families', in R.H. Mikesell, D.D. Lusterman and S.H. McDaniel (eds) *Integrating Family Therapy: Handbook of Family Psychology and Systems Theory*, Washington, DC: American Psychological Association.

Smyer, M.A., Cohn, M.D. and Brannon, D. (1988) *Mental Health Consultation in Nursing Homes*, New York: New York University Press.

Spark, G.M. and Brody, E.M. (1970) 'The aged are family members', *Family Process*, 9: 195–210.

Treacher, A. (1995) 'Reviewing consumer studies of therapy: family therapy research', in S. Reimers and A. Treacher (eds) *Introducing User-friendly Family Therapy*, London: Routledge.

Walsh, F. (1989) 'The family in later life', in B. Carter and M.C. McGoldrick (eds) *The Changing Family Life Cycle: A Framework for Family Therapy*, Boston: Allyn & Bacon.

Zarit, S.H. and Edwards, A.B. (1996) 'Family caregiving: research and clinical intervention', in R.T. Woods (ed.) *Handbook of the Clinical Psychology of Ageing*, London: Wiley.

Zarit, S.H. and Whitlatch, C.J. (1992) 'Institutional placement: phases of the transition'. *The Gerontologist*, 32: 665–672.

Chapter 5

Interpersonal psychotherapy

Mark D. Miller and Charles F. Reynolds III

Historical background

Interpersonal Psychotherapy (IPT) is a focused, short-term, manual-based psychotherapy designed to be implemented by a variety of healthcare professionals. Its original application was with depression although further applications have since been developed. Klerman, Weissman, Rounsaville *et al.* developed the techniques of IPT (Klerman *et al.* 1984, Weissman *et al.* 2000) after making the following observations. First, that depression in any individual impacts their interpersonal relationships regardless of the cause of the depression; second, that a focus on the current interpersonal relationships of a depressed individual is an efficient and systematizable means of rapidly assessing their coping difficulty in a forum for change, greater hopefulness and remission of depressive symptoms. Klerman *et al.* also observed that most themes in psychotherapy fall into one of four broad categories: unresolved grief, role transition, role dispute or interpersonal deficits. A clearly defined focus serves to keep the patient/therapist dyad working on a limited, more manageable problem area with a greater chance of achieving mastery in a brief time. Klerman *et al.* have shown that a predefined, limited number of weekly sessions is adequate to address most focal issues in psychotherapy. They also point out that the awareness of impending termination in a short-term psychotherapy is a conscious and unconscious motivator for patients to continue working in therapy.

The theoretical framework of IPT arose from several lines of empirical investigation, most notably the interpersonal school of psychiatry that developed in the Baltimore/Washington area of the United States early in the twentieth century. Adolf Meyer, the former chairman of the psychiatry department at Johns Hopkins

University, advocated the psychobiological approach to understanding patients, which included an assessment of the individual's reactions to developmental stages and critical life events (Meyer 1957). Harry Stack Sullivan (1953) has been the most prolific writer about interpersonal psychiatry with contributions from Mable Blake Cohen (Cohen *et al.* 1954) and Frieda Fromm-Reichmann (1960), among others. The tenets of attachment theory, as elucidated by John Bowlby and others, also figure prominently in the theoretical underpinnings of IPT. Bowlby studied infants and mothers and noted that the quality of the initial bonding had profound and lifelong effects on the quality of subsequent interpersonal relationships (Bowlby 1977). Poor bonding resulted in an impaired ability to gain satisfaction from interpersonal relationships, often resulting in depression (Bowlby 1969). Henderson *et al.* (1978) found that depressed individuals had fewer friends and supportive relationships. Brown *et al.* (1977) found that a confiding relationship with a male protected females from depression during stressful events. Paykel *et al.* (Paykel *et al.* 1969; Paykel 1978) noted that a stressful social transition often preceded a depressive episode. Weissman and Paykel (1974) further noted that the hostility, poor communication and impairment in social role functioning seen in depressed women, improved with recovery from depression. From these empirical sources, Klerman *et al.* concluded that close interpersonal relationships play an important role in preventing depression and, conversely, that disruption of those relationships can play a causal role in depression. Klerman *et al.* sought to create a psychosocial intervention to address interpersonal issues in a pragmatic and timely way. In their pilot work with depressed patients, these interpersonal stresses were duly noted by the social workers in the research clinic, and a collaborative effort ensued to attempt to systematize techniques for addressing interpersonal difficulties, with the goal of achieving the relief of depressive symptoms. Interpersonal psychotherapy has been demonstrated to be an efficacious treatment in younger adults, as an acute treatment (Elkin *et al.* 1989) and as a maintenance treatment (Frank *et al.* 1990).

Theoretical model

The role of the therapist in IPT is, first, to provide psycho-education about the biopsychosocial components of depression, including the utility of antidepressant medication as a proven effective treatment which might be used singly or in combination with psychotherapy. During the initial sessions, the patient is assigned the 'sick role', and the debilitation from depression is likened to that of a serious medical condition, such as pneumonia, in which case the patient would certainly allow themselves to be excused from some or all of their usual responsibilities until they were feeling improved enough to resume them. The IPT therapist provides explicit explanations about the proposed mechanisms of IPT, which include clarification, confrontation, communication analysis and decision analysis. Agreement is solicited from potential patients to comply with weekly attendance, open communication, and a willingness to explore potentially uncomfortable emotional experiences, with the goal being a reduction in symptoms of depression. In addition, potential patients need to agree to abide by the short-term nature of the therapy (12 to 20 weekly sessions).

In order to systematically characterize all relevant interpersonal relationships in the patient's sphere, the second task of IPT is to conduct an interpersonal inventory. This inventory is undertaken within the first two sessions by soliciting from the patient personalized descriptions of all family members, lovers, friends, co-workers and community contacts who play any relevant role in the patient's life. This completed picture allows the IPT therapist to broadly assess the manner in which the depressive symptoms are manifested in the interpersonal relationships of the patient, and to begin to look for ways in which new strategies might improve patterns of interaction that are unsatisfying or maladaptive.

Within the first three sessions, the patient has been extensively educated about depression, including the possible concomitant need for antidepressant medication, and the methods utilized in IPT, including planned termination after 12 to 20 sessions. The IPT therapist has constructed a detailed map of all relevant interpersonal relationships of the patient. By the second or third IPT session, the IPT therapist has amassed enough data regarding the chief complaint, general functioning, and interpersonal relationships of the patient, to formulate a focus, which is presented to the patient for discussion. A jointly agreed-upon focus is thus established for commencing the therapeutic work. Using communication analysis, clarification, confrontation and decision analysis, the IPT therapist seeks to elucidate all aspects of the agreed-upon focus within the patient's environment and the interpersonal relationships contained therein. Alternative strategies for coping are explored, and patients are encouraged to be open to trying new strategies between sessions and reviewing the outcome in subsequent sessions.

Excluding any new crisis that demands attention, the role of the IPT therapist is to see that the agreed focus is maintained, with the emphasis on problem-solving in the here-and-now. The role of the IPT therapist is to repeatedly return the attention of the patient to current interpersonal relationships, while acknowledging past traumas or early-life conflictual relationships. In-depth exploration of early-life events is purposely avoided as these cannot be addressed in short-term therapy. Instead, problem-solving is used to address residual maladaptive coping patterns that occur in the here-and-now. Similarly, transference interpretations are avoided, with the exception of an intense negative transference threatening to breach treatment.

In a short-term psychotherapy such as IPT, the therapist begins thinking about a termination strategy as soon as the patient is considered to be a suitable candidate. Observations from psycho-analysis indicate that termination can be a lengthy and difficult pro-cess, to work through the attachment that the patient develops towards the therapist. In IPT, this complication is purposely minim-ized by repeatedly deflecting any transference-laden utterances of the patient on to similar situations the patient has described in their interpersonal relationships in the real world. Positive transferential comments, or small gifts, are accepted with politeness, but the IPT therapist does not ask the patient how they feel about their therapist or encourage more in-depth exploration of transference feelings. When the patient has been directed all along to look to their inter-personal relationships and to find the support they need in the real world, an easier transition during termination is possible.

The four broad foci of IPT are particularly appropriate for prob-lems commonly faced by the elderly. The risk of losing a family member, or other valued interpersonal contact, increases with age, and unresolved grief over a particular loss can result. Role transi-tions are common events for elders, such as retirement, children moving away, selling a home, or coping with new disability or dependency as a result of medical problems. Role disputes can occur at any age, but advancing age does not offer any particular protection. In our experience, marital disputes can become more problematic with age, as declining health or increasing dependence in one partner can increase distress, resentment and feelings of hopelessness in the other. Also, the option of leaving a conflictual marriage is perceived by many elders to be less of an option, sometimes leading to a greater sense of hopelessness in a dysfunctional marriage. In research trials with older adults, the most frequent focus is role transition, followed by interpersonal dispute, then abnormal grief and interpersonal deficit. One half of elderly patients merit two foci during IPT.

Interpersonal deficits are defined as chronic difficulties in finding satisfying interpersonal relationships. This focus often includes individuals with significant character psychopathology. In the IPT manual, this category is also the catch-all category when a particular patient's problem doesn't fit well into any of the other three categories. Elderly individuals whose problems are best captured in this focus often face increasing difficulties in their maladaptive coping strategies with advancing age, particularly if illness or disability forces them into greater dependency on others.

Applications of interpersonal therapy and selection of patients

It is noteworthy in the *Comprehensive Guide to Interpersonal Psychotherapy* (Weissman *et al.* 2000) that there are no selection guidelines for inclusion in IPT. Of course, all psychotherapies, as the American psychotherapist Judd Marmar once said, have three things in common. There must be:

1 Rapport.
2 Some motivation on the part of the patient to seek relief from pain or distress.
3 An expectation that the therapist has some expertise, that is, something to offer that promises to be potentially helpful.

The selection criteria for IPT certainly meet this broad definition. The tenor of the published reports of IPT lean towards all-inclusiveness rather than selectivity, perhaps due to the fact that IPT has been used extensively in research trials where inclusion criteria generally include minimum levels of symptom severity, but in which exclusions are generally limited to substance abuse, psychosis, or severe medical illness. In the Pittsburgh Maintenance Therapies in Late-Life Depression Study, for example, dementia was an exclusion criterion in the original study by requiring a Folstein Mini-Mental Status (MMSE) score of 27 or greater for inclusion (Folstein *et al.* 1975). In an ongoing follow-up study, however, we have broadened our inclusion criteria to include moderately demented, depressed subjects with MMSE scores of 15 or greater in order to provide more generalizable results which reflect the typical range of the geriatric population.

We have not found that any major modifications of IPT are required in working with older adults. At times, we have utilized shorter sessions for patients with agitated depression and we have held phone sessions with patients unable to get out due to inclement weather or illness. We have also accepted input from concerned or accompanying family or care-providers when appropriate. Although we encountered a range of psychological mindedness in our research participants, even those with little formal education were able to learn from the educational component of IPT and, with rare exceptions, were able to comply with and benefit from IPT.

Although IPT was specifically developed for the treatment of uni-polar depression, it has been adapted for use in a wider range of disorders, including dysthymic disorder (Markowitz 1997), main-tenance treatment in recurrent major depression (Frank *et al.* 1991), conjoint therapy in marital disputes (Foley *et al.* 1989), bipolar disorder (Frank *et al.* 2000) and anxiety disorders (Lipsitz *et al.* 1999). It also has applications in consultation-liaison psychiatry, including depression following myocardial infarction (Stuart and Cole 1996), body dysmorphic disorder (Veale *et al.* 1996) and somatization disorder (Scott and Ikkos 1996). In working with somatization disorder patients, treatment-seeking is conceptualized as an interpersonal issue. After establishing a therapeutic alliance, the initial aim of therapy is to help the patient cope with their physical problems. Thereafter, interactions with physicians can be discussed using role-play to illustrate how hostile feelings and excessive demands can lead to unsatisfactory help-seeking (S. Scott, University of Iowa, personal communication). IPT is also being developed to help patients with Alzheimer's disease.

The presence of personality disorder pathology is not an exclu-sion for IPT. There is no attempt to restructure personality in IPT, although one group (Angus and Gillies 1994) attempted to treat patients with borderline personality disorder with IPT. In our experience, however, those patients with more severe personality disorders often do not consent to psychotherapy or are poorly com-pliant with follow-up. These patients may be better served by a psychotherapy such as 'dialectical behavior therapy' (DBT), developed by Linehan and colleagues (Linehan 1987) and currently being adapted specifically for the elderly by Lynch and colleagues at Duke University in North Carolina (Lynch 2000). DBT was designed specifically for teaching patients techniques to better manage the intense affects, suicidal ideation and dysfunctional behaviours often associated with severe personality disorders.

In summary, any patient with significant symptoms of depression who is willing to engage in the IPT process is a potential candidate. IPT does not require a high degree of formal education, or more than low-average intelligence or any prior therapeutic experience. As IPT provides a great deal of education for patients in the early sessions, patients with no prior experience or understanding of psychotherapy can still benefit and become educated consumers of IPT. Any impediment to regular attendance such as substance abuse, medical illness or severe personality pathology would hinder progress in IPT, as it would for any psychotherapy.

Therapy in practice

Box 5.1 summarizes the application of IPT to depression as developed by Klerman, Weissman *et al.* Originally published as a manual in 1984 and later revised and published (Weissman *et al.* 2000), it is a step-by-step outline of the strategy for applying interpersonal psychotherapy during the initial, intermediate and termination stages of therapy. Upon completion of the interpersonal inventory in the first two sessions, and after hearing the patient's story and account of the extent of their symptoms, the therapist begins to formulate a proposed focus for the therapy in one of four broad categories. Strategies for addressing all four foci (grief, role transition, role dispute, and interpersonal deficit) are included in Box 5.1.

Within the structure of interpersonal therapy illustrated in Box 5.1, a number of techniques are used to gather information and facilitate change. These are now described, as adapted from Weissman *et al.* (2000).

Non-directive exploration

To facilitate relatively free discussion of material, general, open-ended questions are best, especially in the first phase of sessions. The therapist usually begins sessions with the focusing but still open-ended question 'How have things been since we last met?' If

Box 5.1 Outline of interpersonal psychotherapy for major depression

I The initial session

Dealing with the depression
Review depressive symptoms
Give the syndrome a name
Explain depression as a medical illness and explain the treatment
Give the patient the 'sick role'
Evaluate the need for medication

Relate depression to the interpersonal context
Review current and past interpersonal relationships as they relate to
   current depressive symptoms
Determine with the patient the nature of interaction with significant
   persons; expectations of the patient and significant persons
   of one another, and whether these were filled; satisfying
   and unsatisfying aspects of the relationships; and changes the
   patient wants in the relationships

Identification of major problem areas
Determine the problem area related to current depression and set
   the treatment goals
Determine which relationship or aspect of a relationship is related
   to the depression and what might change in it

Explain the IPT concepts and contract
Outline your understanding of the problem
Agree on treatment goals, determining which problem area will be
   the focus
Describe procedures of IPT: here-and-now focus; need for patient to
   discuss important concerns; review of current interpersonal
   relationships; discussion of practical aspects of treatment-
   length, frequency, times, etc.

II Intermediate sessions – the problem areas

Grief

Goals
Facilitate the mourning process
Help the patient to re-establish interest and relationships to
   substitute for what has been lost

Strategies
Review depressive symptoms
Relate symptom onset to death of significant other
Reconstruct the patient's relationship with the deceased
Describe the sequence and consequences of events just prior to,
   during, and after the death
Explore associated feelings (negative as well as positive)
Consider possible ways of becoming involved with others

Interpersonal role disputes

Goals

Identify dispute

Choose plan of action

Modify expectations or faulty communication to bring about a satisfactory resolution

Strategies

Review depressive symptoms

Relate symptom onset to overt or covert dispute with significant other with whom patient is currently involved

Determine stage of dispute:

Renegotiation (calm down participants to facilitate resolution)

Impasse (increase disharmony in order to reopen negotiation)

Dissolution (assist mourning)

Understand how non-reciprocal role expectations relate to dispute:

What are the issues in the dispute?

What are the differences in expectations and values?

What are the options?

What is the likelihood of finding alternatives?

What resources are available to bring about change in the relationship?

Are there parallels in other relationships?

What is the patient thinking?

What unspoken assumptions lie behind the patient's behaviour?

How is the dispute perpetuated?

Role transitions

Goals

Mourning and acceptance of the loss of the old role

Help the patient to regard the new role as more positive

Restore self-esteem by developing a sense of mastery regarding the demands of the new role

Strategies

Review depressive symptoms

Relate depressive symptoms to difficulty in coping with some recent life change

Review positive and negative aspects of old and new roles

Explore feelings about what is lost

Explore feelings about the change itself

Explore opportunities in new role

Realistically evaluate what is lost

Encourage appropriate release of affect

Encourage development of social support system and of new skills called for in new role

Interpersonal deficits
Goals
Reduce the patient's social isolation
Encourage formation of new relationships
Strategies
Review depressive symptoms
Relate depressive symptoms to problems of social isolation or
unfulfilment
Review past significant relationships including their negative and
positive aspects
Explore repetitive patterns in relationships
Discuss patient's positive and negative feelings about therapist and
seek parallels in other relationships

III Termination

Explicit discussion of termination
Acknowledgement that termination is a time of grieving
Moves toward patient recognition of independent competence
Dealing with non-response
Continuation/maintenance treatment

Source: adapted from Weissman *et al.* 2000. Copyright © 2000 by Basic Books.
Reprinted by permission of Basic Books, a member of Perseus Books, L.L.C.

material is being discussed in a productive way, non-directive techniques can be used to encourage the patient to continue talking.
These techniques include *supportive acknowledgement* (nodding,
or saying 'Mm-hm', 'I see', 'Please continue'), *extension of the topic
discussed* (in which the therapist directly encourages the patient to
continue on an initiated subject), and *receptive silence* (in which the
therapist maintains an interested and attentive attitude).

Direct elicitation

Direct elicitation is best used to obtain a thorough evaluation of a
particular problem area and to check the therapist's interpersonal
hypotheses. Specific questions should be asked only with some purpose in mind, such as to help the patient see his or her role in a
situation, to develop a database, or to elicit an avoided affect, and
only in some semblance of flow from where the discussion has
moved. Too much skipping around and too many specific, closed
questions should be avoided.

Encouragement of affect and acceptance of painful affect

Encouragement of affect denotes a number of therapeutic techniques which are intended to help the patient express, understand, and manage emotion. The relatively free expression of affect in psychotherapy distinguishes it from other relationships, in which affective components are often highly constricted. The learning in therapy is an emotional learning, and dealing with affect is essential in bringing about changes. In developing new interpersonal strategies, the elicitation of affect about others may help patients to decide on priorities and strive toward emotionally meaningful goals.

Many patients need help with acceptance of affect such as excessive guilt feelings related to strong, hostile or sexual feelings about significant others. They may be only partly aware of such emotions. For example, an important aspect of distorted or delayed grief reactions is often unacceptable to the patient. When the patient gives evidence of painful, unacknowledged, or suppressed feelings of this sort, the therapist's job is to encourage the clear expression of the affect. Some patients are emotionally constricted or have maladaptive lack of emotion in situations in which strong affects are normally felt. They may be so unassertive that they do not feel anger when their rights are violated by others. Some patients may feel anger but lack the courage to express it in assertive behaviour. Others may not feel anger because it has never occurred to them that others should act differently towards them. With these patients, it may be useful to point out that they are being abused. Patients who have difficulty feeling and expressing other types of feelings such as affection, gratitude, or caring may be helped to discover irrational fears that led to the suppression of these emotions.

Use of affects in interpersonal relationships

Some schools of psychotherapy hold the belief that the best way to manage affects is to express them in a cathartic fashion. In IPT the expression of strong feelings in the therapeutic session is seen as an important starting point for much therapeutic work, but their expression outside the session is not a goal in itself. Since the goal is to help the patient act more effectively in interpersonal relationships, this may involve either expressing or suppressing affects, depending on the circumstances. The IPT therapist may help the patient to manage her affective experience in several ways. First, the patient and the significant other may negotiate to bring about changes that eliminate the circumstances that evoke painful feelings. For example, a patient who feels repeated disappointment and anger with a spouse's behaviour may not feel this way if the behaviour changes. Second, the patient may learn to avoid painful situations when appropriate. A third way of managing affect is to delay expressing it or acting on it until one has calmed down. This might include strategies such as planning with a spouse to postpone an argument until a time when both have achieved some distance on the matter to be discussed.

A fourth way of changing painful affects is to help patients to revise their thinking about an affect-laden topic, so that the emotion that arises in response to this thinking is also revised. This cognitive strategy is particularly important in the management of anxiety. Depressed patients frequently have high levels of anxiety in relation to irrational thoughts and fears. By exposing the irrational thoughts and helping the patient to arrive at alternative ways of understanding a situation, the therapist may help to reduce anxiety. Anger can also be mitigated through revising the patient's understanding of the situation in which anger arose. Often this revised understanding involves a more mature acceptance of unchangeable circumstances.

Clarification

The therapist uses clarification to restructure and feed back the patient's material. The immediate purpose is to make the patient more aware of what has actually been communicated. In the longer term, this may facilitate the patient's discussion of previously suppressed material. Specific techniques for clarification are listed.

- *Asking patients to repeat or rephrase what they have said.* This is particularly useful if the patient has made a mis-statement, said something in a surprising or unusual way, or contradicted previous statements.
- *Rephrasing what the patient has said* and asking what was intended. The rephrasing should be done in a way that places the patient's statement in an interpersonal context. For instance, a patient discussing an incident in which his wife had come home late described his feelings by saying 'There was anger', to which the therapist replied 'You were angry with her?'
- *Calling attention to the logical extension of a statement that the*

patient has made or pointing out implicit assumptions in what was said.

- *Calling the patient's attention to contrasts or contradictions* in her presentation of material is the most useful clarification technique. Contradictions may be noted between the patient's affect expression and the verbal discussion of a topic. Discrepancies can be noted over time when the same material is brought up. Contrasts can be seen between a statement of intentions and overt behaviour, or between the patient's statements of goals and the limitations of reality. It is important to confront the patient with these contradictory statements in a spirit of enquiry and not in an accusatory fashion. Contradictions can be pointed out by queries such as 'Isn't it interesting that you said X, while previously you said Y?' or 'What can we make of the contrast between what you said and [what you said before]?'

- *Restating statements by the patient that imply a pervasive, unhelpful belief or thought.* Some people, for example, have a habit of thinking in extremes, particularly when they are depressed. From a patient's discussion of his or her work, the therapist may note that the patient thinks that he or she is either a total success or an utter failure, without gradations in between, pointing this out as a depressive distortion which is likely to resolve as they work together on treating the depression. Unlike cognitive therapy, however, these irrational thoughts are not specifically catalogued, tested, and challenged. Instead, the therapist simply describes these thoughts as symptoms of the depression episode which are interfering with the patient's interpersonal functioning.

Communication analysis

Communication analysis is used to examine and identify communication failures in order to help the patient learn to communicate more effectively. Specifically, the therapist seeks out problems in communication by asking for a highly detailed account of an important conversation or argument the patient has had with a significant other. This reconstruction of the interpersonal event should attempt both a verbatim 'transcript' of the interaction and a description of the patient's feelings and intentions at critical points. Some common communication difficulties are listed.

- *Ambiguous, indirect nonverbal communication as a substitute for open confrontation.* Verbal communication has many advantages over nonverbal communication in terms of its explicitness and understandability. Many patients who either distrust verbal communication or fear openly expressing their feelings or thoughts rely on nonverbal communication or actions to get their point across to others. They may sulk when angry or make suicidal gestures when they feel lonely or deprived. The person to whom these actions are addressed cannot know what is being asked or how best to respond.
- *Incorrect assumption that one has communicated.* Many people assume that others will know their needs or feelings without their having to make themselves clear, expecting the other person to anticipate their wants or, in effect, be a mindreader. ('Of course he knows what I think.') This often results in anger and frustration, again silent and unexpressed. Other people, having tried to communicate a message, do not bother to make sure that they have been heard or understood.
- *Incorrect assumption that one has understood.* Many depressed patients fear massive retaliation or criticism from others and are afraid to ask if what was perceived as criticism was actually intended that way.
- *Unnecessarily indirect verbal communication.* Many depressed patients are highly inhibited about directly expressing quite reasonable expectations or criticisms of others. As a result, they may build up resentments about being mistreated by a person who is unaware of having given offence. Instead of direct communication, the patient may use hints or ambiguous messages.
- *Silence – closing off communication.* Many patients have discovered that silence can be an effective and infuriating way of handling a disagreement with others, but they may be unaware of the destructive potential of closing off communications entirely.

Use of the therapeutic relationship

In this technique, the patient's feelings about the therapist and/or the therapy become the focus of discussion. Thoughts, feelings, expectations, and behaviour in the therapeutic relationship are examined in so far as they represent a model of the patient's characteristic ways of feeling and/or behaving in other relationships. If the focus is role disputes, feedback is given on how a person comes across to others, helping the patient to understand pathological interactions by re-experiencing them with the therapist, but going one step further and solving them. If the focus is grief and loss, reactions to the therapist may show how the patient has cut off from others or developed relationships that mirror the one with the lost person. With interpersonal deficits the patient develops a relationship with the therapist as a model for other relationships.

Behaviour change techniques

Lasting improvement from depression usually depends on changes in the patient's interpersonal behaviour outside therapy. In IPT, the therapist can use directive techniques including education, advice, modelling, or helping the patient to solve relatively simple, practical problems. In establishing a positive working relationship in the early phases of treatment, the therapist should be alert to the possibility of directly helping the patient to solve such practical problems as finding transportation, housing, or public financial assistance. Since the goal of treatment is to help the patient to function independently, heavy use of direct assistance or advice is to be avoided. Rather, patients should be taught to analyse new situations for themselves and make their own choices. As an overall strategy, the therapist should move from relatively direct helping toward relatively indirect helping as treatment progresses. Advice and suggestions should be provided only when the therapist thinks the patient is unable to make a successful decision on her own. Limit-setting may be necessary for highly impulsive individuals whose behaviour is destructive either to themselves or to the treatment. The therapist may choose to demand that the patient refrain from a given behaviour if she is to remain in treatment.

Education is an essential function of IPT. Ultimately, all the interventions of IPT are aimed at educating patients about their interactions with others. Education is preferred to advice-giving in that it is aimed at providing the patient with the skills with which to make her own choices. Modelling may also be employed. This is similar to advice-giving, because it involves giving the patient examples of how the therapist has handled problems similar to the patient's. This technique is helpful in conveying to patients that they are not unique in having difficulties and that others have succeeded in solving their problems.

Decision analysis

This is a technique by which the patient is helped to consider a wide range of alternative actions (and their consequences) that can be taken to solve a given problem. This is a major action-oriented technique of IPT and should be explicitly taught to the patient for use outside treatment. It often follows communication analysis. Many depressed patients have a history of making self-defeating decisions, partly because they fail to consider all reasonable alternatives and to evaluate the consequences of their actions. The role of the therapist in decision analysis is to help the patient recognize a broadening range of options and to insist that action be held off until each option is adequately explored.

Role-play

This is used to accomplish two important tasks: first, exploration of the patient's feelings and style of communication with others; and second, rehearsal of new ways for the patient to behave with others. For the first task, role-playing can be used when the therapist feels that patients are not adequately conveying a sense of their relationships with others. When a therapist pretends to be the other person, the patient may react in fresh and revealing ways. For the second task, role-play can be used to train the patient to interact with others in new ways, such as being more assertive or expressing anger. It is a great leap to go from thinking about acting differently to actually doing so. Often the patient has been aware for years of a desire or need to change but has been unable to do so. Role-play allows the patient to practise in a safe setting and thus may provide for a smoother transition from plans to action.

Contract setting

This refers to the sequence of semi-structured tasks in the initial session(s) which are aimed at educating the patient about IPT and obtaining the patient's cooperation as a partner in the therapeutic work. Tasks include an individualized explanation of the IPT rationale, an explanation of IPT techniques, some communication to the patient about the therapist's understanding of what brings the patient into therapy, and a discussion of the practical dimensions of treatment (length of sessions, frequency, duration of therapy, appointment time, missed sessions policy, fee, etc.).

Two case histories are now presented to illustrate the application of IPT with depressed older patients.

Case illustration 1: Miss Edwards
Therapeutic foci: abnormal grief and role dispute

Miss Edwards, a 64-year-old, white, single female, reported a three-year history of persistent depressive symptoms. She had never married, but was very close to her siblings and their families. Miss Edwards was a retired healthcare professional and regularly assumed the role of care-giver with her extended family. She was particularly close to her numerous nephews and enjoyed playing golf with them. Four years earlier, one nephew had died of leukemia at age 37. A month after this tragic event, another nephew died suddenly from a cerebral aneurysm. Two brothers died subsequently and a great-nephew (age 25) died in a car accident. Miss Edwards opened with the sentence, 'I have been grieving for the last four years.' To make matters worse, due to her history of breast cancer treatment, colon resection, and recent carpal tunnel surgery, she could not play golf for an entire season, which further depressed her.

Miss Edwards's initial IPT focus was abnormal grief. Her grief was complicated by the fact that she resented being continually thrust into the role of liaison with various healthcare providers who were caring for her ill relatives. She found this obligation to be extremely stressful. Additionally, while other family members received support and acknowledgement of their losses, no one, she felt, recognized the depth of her own loss. She was 'only the aunt'. Miss Edwards's situation has been characterized in the literature as 'disenfranchised grief' (Doka 1996).

By first acknowledging the legitimacy of her grief, IPT offered Miss Edwards the opportunity to finally grieve, to talk about how she experienced her nephews' and brothers' deaths, not only as the family nurse but also as their beloved aunt. The build-up of resentment about family assumptions that she would automatically take on the role of liaison on medical matters was designated a secondary IPT focus of role dispute. Learning to set limits and sometimes to 'just say no' were discussed at length and put into practice during her course of IPT. Once the component of role dispute was satisfactorily resolved by Miss Edwards developing the determination to stop short-changing her own needs in light of the needs of others, she was able to fully experience and work through her grief in the safety and supportive environment of her IPT sessions.

Discussion of Mrs Edwards

The IPT method of handling abnormal grief is to facilitate the mourning process and help the patient re-establish interests and relationships to substitute for the loss. The IPT therapist relates the patient's depressive symptoms to the loss, explores the lost relation-ship in detail along with the associated feelings (negative as well as positive) and, finally, explores the sequences of events surrounding the death and the resultant personalized consequences for the patient. In this vignette, Mrs Edwards needed help to recognize that she was entitled to her own grief as much as any other family mem-ber, and she was able to acknowledge that continuing her role as dispenser of medical advice and care-giving to the rest of the family was untenable for her.

For further discussions about the use of IPT in spousal, bereavement-related depression, see Miller *et al.* 1994.

Case illustration 2: Mrs Jackson
Therapeutic foci: role transition and role dispute

Mrs Jackson, a 65-year-old, white, married female, presented in her fourth episode of major depression, never having had any previous experience in psychotherapy. She presented with several psycho-social stressors, most prominently recent retirement. She was extremely anxious and guarded at the onset of therapy, and reported an almost complete remission of depressive symptoms in the first week. Within several weeks, however, her symptoms returned to their original severity. Mrs Jackson was quite anxious and had a difficult time engaging actively in therapy. After an ini-tially cautious start, the educational component of IPT appeared to pay off, and she began to engage more actively. Gradually, she began talking about her difficulties in adjusting to retirement. These difficulties included time management, learning to manage money, and setting boundaries on her availability for baby-sitting her grandchildren. The first five to eight sessions focused on these role transition issues.

Once Mrs Jackson began to feel somewhat better and as her trust in her therapist deepened, she began to reveal more deep-seated resentments and conflicts towards her husband. She requested that the focus shift away from her problems with retirement on to her conflicts with him. She stated that she was now willing to examine her own feelings and behaviours and work on ways to try to make life better with her husband. She grappled with many long-standing conflicts with him. Each situation that she brought to light manifested an underlying imbalance of power and control. Mrs Jackson described her husband as a benign dictator, but a dictator none the less. In exploring these issues in IPT, she concluded that she must try to speak up more, and to be more clear about her needs. Initially, this created more conflict as well as intense internal dissonance. She eventually began to recognize her own responsibility in allowing her husband to control even minor decisions, and she recognized that it was not easy for her to assert herself. As her IPT therapist encouraged her to try alternative strategies, she was both surprised and delighted to find that her husband was more willing to share in decision-making than she thought possible. With practice, she eventually became more comfortable in this newly acquired role. Through her active participation in IPT, Mrs. Jackson made healthy adjustments to retirement, and reduced the role disputes that chronically characterized her marriage. Her depression which had resulted from feeling hopelessly stuck was resolved.

Discussion of Mrs Jackson

The definition of a role dispute is a non-reciprocal interpersonal expectation. If the patient feels that the dispute is unresolvable, a fall in self-esteem can result and become a nidus for depression. The IPT therapist attempts to help the patient to determine the stage of the dispute, that is, whether to pursue a course of:

1   Renegotiation, by calming the participants.
2   Increasing disharmony to break an impasse.
3   Assisting in mourning for a relationship that is in the dissolution phase.

In Mrs Jackson's case, it appeared that she was willing to try renegotiation by first examining her own role in maintaining an imbalance of power and control. Recognizing this impediment to better marital collaboration, Mrs Jackson's therapist used techniques of clarification, confrontation, and communication analysis to clearly identify the problem and subsequently to explore, devise, test and practise strategies that required Mrs Jackson to selectively assert her will more effectively. It has been our experience, in systematically applying IPT to 180 elderly patients, that the initial focus of role transition often resolves only to reveal more long-standing role disputes, usually spousal. A role transition produces a crisis in the status quo of a given interpersonal relationship which becomes the presenting complaint; but as work in IPT progresses, rapport and trust deepen such that the more chronic and difficult problems of role dispute come to the fore.

Mrs Jackson presented with difficulties in her adjustment to retirement and was similar to the case of Mrs Edwards in her difficulty setting limits and taking care of herself in light of her pattern of devotion to the needs of others. Through confrontation and clarification in IPT, Mrs Jackson gradually consented to begin work on role disputes with her husband, although initially she was very pessimistic that change was possible. Systematically exploring her role by analysing their communication and helping her to see that her posture towards her husband was a choice that she could decide to alter, was a breakthrough for her. Exploring alternative methods worked well, and her confidence rose with the feeling that she could 'pick her battles' and insist on some changes being made. Her progress brought relief of feelings of despair and hopelessness and, through maintenance IPT sessions, it is not difficult to predict that reinforcing and continually clarifying these gains had a protective effect against a recurrence of depression for Mrs Jackson.

Case illustration 3: Mr Lewis
Therapeutic foci: role transition and role dispute

Mr Lewis was a 61-year-old, white, married professional who presented in his third episode of major depression, superimposed on a baseline of dysthymia. Two prior episodes had been successfully treated with antidepressant medication. He reported seeing a psychiatrist previously for advice about what to do with his life during a mid-life crisis, but had not found it to be very helpful.

While obtaining the social inventory during the first sessions of IPT, several psychosocial stressors were revealed. His son, who was unemployed and had a history of drug abuse and antisocial behaviour, had announced that he was moving back home after an unsuccessful attempt to find employment. Mr Lewis and his wife were unsure about how they would handle their son upon his return. However worrisome his son's situation was to him, a more pressing issue had to do with his professional practice. His partner had recently retired, leaving him with an office he could not afford. Gradually, a picture came into focus of a man with deep ambivalence about his chosen profession and a pattern of financial negligence in paying debts and collecting fees which was nearly bankrupting him. Mr Lewis was very explicit in stating that he was depressed because he couldn't come to a decision about whether to continue his practice, find other employment, or retire early. A focus on role transition seemed most appropriate at the outset. After exploring several options, and providing him with the opportunity to ventilate his feelings about his work, he finally decided, with much trepidation, to invest in a new office. He found a young partner, and opened a new practice. His goal was to retire in five years. His depression gradually improved over the ensuing months.

The focus of IPT then shifted to role dispute as his son had moved home and showed little ambition or initiative in finding a new job. Eventually, he and his wife decided to give their son a deadline for finding a job, or moving out. His wife ended up being the primary enforcer of the deadline, illustrating Mr Lewis's pattern of passive behaviour. Unfortunately, during his course of IPT, Mr Lewis's wife was diagnosed with cancer. She was successfully treated with chemotherapy and achieved a rapid remission, but her tolerance of her husband's behaviour was diminishing, and she became more confrontational. Mr Lewis's long-standing pattern of 'forgetting' to fulfil his responsibilities now seemed more pronounced, as his wife's treatment had left her greatly weakened and more of the day-to-day responsibility of running their affairs fell into his hands. One day, she telephoned out of desperation, complaining about his behaviour in light of their dire financial circumstances. A few conjoint sessions were deemed necessary to deal with this crisis. During these sessions, Mr Lewis did not deny his wife's accusations of a long-standing pattern of passive-aggressive behaviour and convenient forgetfulness. The inclusion of his wife in these conjoint sessions helped to more fully reveal the patient's lifelong passive-aggressive character pathology. His forgetfulness became so problematic that Mr Lewis and his wife requested neuropsychological testing because they were afraid that he might be showing early signs of dementia. The test results were negative for significant cognitive impairment.

Since IPT does not seek to change personality structure, the IPT focused, in a very practical way, on the tasks at hand. Mr Lewis's day-to-day responsibilities were reviewed during his IPT sessions, and he appeared to be honest and somewhat embarrassed in discussing the duties he had failed to complete. He learned to take more responsibility for the running of the household, and became more attentive to his wife's needs, and more honest with her about what he was willing and able to do.

Discussion of Mr Lewis

The case of Mr Lewis consisted of three role transitions:

1   His work crisis.
2   His son's return home.
3   His wife's diagnosis of cancer.

A secondary focus of role dispute ensued when his wife confronted him regarding his long-standing pattern of irresponsibility, particularly in her time of need for greater support. This case illustrates the flexibility of IPT to include joint sessions when a crisis is at hand and to use those sessions to further the goals and understanding of the patient's individual focus in IPT. Clarification, decision analysis, confrontation, and communication analysis were all utilized by Mr Lewis's IPT therapist, to facilitate a thorough understanding of his difficulties and to help him to see the way in which his coping style was no longer working effectively within his marriage. Although IPT does not set goals for character change, the forces at work in Mr Lewis's life were causing him to make changes. IPT helped him to see his situation more clearly and to acquire better methods to work at his problems more successfully. IPT also provided a forum to review his progress over time and make further adjustments.

Summary

Interpersonal therapy is a time-limited therapy which focuses on current interpersonal relationships, not intrapsychic conflicts. Personality factors are recognized but not focused upon. IPT deals with the present rather than the distant past. The role of the IPT therapist is one of an empathetic facilitator for maintaining the focus of IPT and for redirecting the therapeutic work on to interpersonal relationships in the real world. In our experience, IPT is a form of psychotherapy ideally suited for use with elderly depressed patients. It does not require that the patient have a high level of education or prior psychotherapy experience or a high degree of psychological mindedness. Despite the fact that patients do not come seeking psychotherapy *per se*, it has been our experience that the vast majority of subjects are able to learn from the psycho-educational component of IPT and become cooperative partners in the interpersonal psychotherapy process. IPT is now being applied to an increasing range of clinical disorders and there is a compelling body of evidence to suggest that IPT in combination with antidepressant treatment is a potent combination in the treatment of late-life depression (see Chapter 7).

Acknowledgements

The authors wish to acknowledge supportive grant funding from the National Institute of Mental Health (USA) MH 43832, MH24652, MH52247, NARSAD, as well as the IPT therapists, Lin Ehrenpreis, Julie Malloy, Jean Picone, Rebecca Silberman, and Lee Wolfson, with supervision by Cleon Cornes, MD, Ellen Frank, Ph.D. and Stanley Imber, Ph.D.

Further reading

For interested patients

Weissman, M.M (1995) *Mastering Depression: A Patient's Guide to Interpersonal Psychotherapy*, Albany, NY: Graywind.

Therapy manual

Weissman, M.M., Markowitz, J.C. and Klerman, G.C. (2000) *Comprehensive Guide to Interpersonal Psychotherapy*, New York: Basic Books.

References

Angus, L. and Gillies, L.A. (1994) 'Counseling the borderline client: an interpersonal approach', *Canadian Journal of Counseling* 28: 69–82.

Bowlby, J. (1969) *Attachment and Loss, Vol. I: Attachment*, London: Hogarth Press.

Bowlby, J. (1977) 'The making and breaking of affectional bonds II: some principles of psychotherapy', *British Journal of Psychiatry* 130: 421–431.

Brown, G.W., Harris, T. and Copeland, J.R. (1977) 'Depression and Loss', *British Journal of Psychiatry*, 130: 1–18.

Cohen, M.B., Baker, G., Cohen, R.A. *et al.* (1954) 'An intensive study of twelve cases of manic depressive psychosis', *Psychiatry* 17: 103–137.

Doka, K.J. (1996) *Living with Grief After Sudden Loss: Suicide, Homicide, Accident, Heart Attack, Stroke*, London: Taylor & Francis.

Elkin, I., Shea, M.T., Watkins, J.T. *et al.* (1989) 'National Institute of Mental Health treatment of depression collaborative research program: general effectiveness of treatments', *Archives of General Psychiatry* 46: 971–982.

Foley, S.H., Rousaville, B.J., Weissman, M.M. *et al.* (1989) 'Individual versus conjoint interpersonal psychotherapy for depressed patients with marital disputes', *International Journal of Family Psychiatry* 10: 29–42.

Frank, E., Kupfer, D.J., Perel, J.M. *et al.* (1990) 'Three-year outcomes for maintenance therapies in recurrent depression', *Archives of General Psychiatry* 47: 1093–1099.

Folstein, M.F., Folstein, S.E. and McHugh, P.R. (1975) 'Mini-mental state examination. A practical method for grading the cognitive state of patients for the clinician', *Journal of Psychiatric Research* 12(3): 189–198.

Frank, E., Kupfer, D.J., Wagner, E.F. *et al.* (1991) 'Efficacy of interpersonal psychotherapy as a maintenance treatment of recurrent depression', *Archives of General Psychiatry* 48: 1053–1059.

Frank, E., Swartz, H.A. and Kupfer, D.J. (2000) 'Interpersonal and social rhythm therapy: managing the chaos of bipolar disorder', *Biological Psychiatry* 48: 593–604.

Fromm-Reichmann, F. (1960) *Principles of Intensive Psychotherapy*, Chicago: Phoenix Books.

Henderson, S., Duncan-Jones, P., McAuley, H. and Ritchie, K. (1978) 'The patient's primary group', *British Journal of Psychiatry* 132: 74–86.

Klerman, G.L. and Weissman, M.M. (1993) *New Applications of Interpersonal Psychotherapy*, Washington DC: American Psychiatric Press.

Klerman, G.L., Weissman, M.M., Rounsaville, B.J. *et al.* (1984) *Interpersonal Psychotherapy of Depression*, New York: Basic Books.

Linehan, M. (1987) 'Dialectical behavior therapy for borderline personality disorder: theory and method', *Bulletin of the Merringer Clinic* 51: 261–276.

Lipsitz, J.D., Fyer, A.J., Markowitz, J.C. and Cherry, S. (1999) 'Open trial of interpersonal psychotherapy for the treatment of social phobia', *American Journal of Psychiatry* 156(11): 1814–1816.

Lynch, T.R. (in press) 'Treatment of elderly depression with personality disorder comorbidity using dialectical behavior therapy', *Cognitive and Behavioral Practice* 7(4): 468–477.

Markowitz, J.C. (1997) *Interpersonal Psychotherapy for Dysthymic Disorder*, Washington, DC: American Psychiatric Press.

Meyer, A. (1957) *Psychobiology: A Science of Man*, Springfield, Ill.: C.C. Thomas.

Miller, M.D., Frank, E., Cornes, C. *et al.* (1994) 'Applying interpersonal psychotherapy to bereavement-related depression following loss of spouse in late-life', *Journal of Psychotherapy Practice and Research* 3: 149–162.

Paykel, E.S. (1978) 'Recent life events in the development of depressive disorder', in R.A. Defue (ed.) *The Psychobiology of the Depressive Disorders: Implications for the Effects of Stress*, New York: Academic Press.

Paykel, E.S., Myers, J.K., Dienelt, M.N., Klerman, G.L., Lindenthal, J.J. and Pepper, M.P. (1969) 'Life events and depression: a controlled study', *Archives of General Psychiatry* 21: 753–760.

Scott, J. and Ikkos, G. (1996) 'A pilot study of interpersonal psychotherapy for the treatment of chronic somatization in primary care.' Presented at First Congress of the World Council of Psychotherapy, June 30, 1996, Vienna, Austria.

Stuart, S. and Cole, V. (1996) 'Treatment of depression following myocardial infarction with interpersonal psychotherapy', *Annals of Clinical Psychiatry* 8(4): 2030.

Sullivan, H.S. (1953) *The Interpersonal Theory of Psychotherapy (TLDP)*, New York: Norton.

Veale, D., Boocock, A., Gournay, K., *et al.* (1996) 'Body dysmorphic disorder. A survey of fifty cases', *British Journal of Psychiatry* 169(2): 196–201.

Weissman, M.M. and Paykel, E.S. (1974) *The Depressed Woman: A Study of Social Relationships*, Chicago: University of Chicago Press.

Weissman, M.M., Markowitz, J.C., Klerman, G.L. *et al* (2000) *Comprehensive Guide to Interpersonal Psychotherapy*, New York: Basic Books.

Chapter 6

Cognitive analytic therapy

Jason Hepple

Historical background

CAT today

Cognitive analytic therapy (CAT) is a time-limited integrative psychotherapy developed in London by Dr Anthony Ryle at St Thomas's and Guy's Hospitals over the last three decades. Driving the evolution of CAT is a desire to develop a unified psychotherapy theory which is grounded in a psychotherapy research base and which can be applied to patients in the context of the modern National Health Service. Its popularity and use have grown steadily, with the umbrella Association for Cognitive Analytic Therapy (ACAT) overseeing training and supervision at many sites in the UK, Europe and beyond, with CAT therapists receiving full United Kingdom Council for Psychotherapy (UKCP) recognition. Developed as a primarily individual psychotherapy, CAT has now been applied to couples, groups and as a systemic tool, and has developed a reputation for containing and helping people with more severe self-destructive and self-harming behaviours.

Ryle (1997) has developed a unique model for understanding borderline personality disorder and traits (as described in DSM-IV), conceptualising the disorder as a primarily dissociative problem, with dramatic shifts occurring between two or more split-off self-states. Following the success of applying this model to a cohort of borderline patients at Guy's (Ryle and Golynkina 2000), there will be a randomised controlled trial of CAT in the treatment of borderline personality disorder.

Sources of CAT

As its name implies, cognitive analytic therapy combines elements of the two major influences on modern-day psychological therapies: cognitive behaviour therapy (CBT) and psychoanalytic psycho-therapy.

CBT has grown out of the discipline of experimental psychology and has its deeper roots in classical and operand conditioning and learning theory. Aaron T. Beck has been the leading figure in the development of clinical applications, and CBT has proved success-ful in treating anxiety-based disorders and mild depression, by describing the links between thoughts, physiology and behaviour. CBT has developed numerous tools to help the client and therapist chart, rate and monitor symptoms, thoughts and actions, so encouraging self-reflection and experimentation with different ways of tackling current problems. A particular influence from the broader cognitive field is the work of George Kelly who developed personal construct theory as a means of charting subjective meaning using the repertory grid technique.

Psychoanalytic psychotherapy has its deep roots in the work of Sigmund Freud and Carl Jung. They developed theories of mind based on the existence of the unconscious (or Id) and the import-ance of repressed memories from early life, and innate drives which generate symptoms and anxiety in the conscious mind (or Ego). These can only be resolved by the bringing of the problematic unconscious material into the conscious realm, through (often lengthy) psychoanalysis. As Freud encapsulated it: 'Where it (Id) was, now am I (Ego).'

CAT has been particularly influenced by the development of Freud's theories by a group known as the object relations theorists, the most influential among these being Melanie Klein and Donald Winnicott. They emphasise the importance of the internalised rela-tionship between the child and the care-givers (or objects), and the processes by which these internal relationships are modified by a cyclical exchange of expectations and gratification or frustration (projection and introjection). It is the internalised relationships rather than the individuals involved in this exchange which act as templates for all future social interaction. Children who have experienced abuse, therefore, are likely to anticipate it in novel others and behave in ways that suggest this – either premature defence or pre-emptive attack. CAT has encapsulated these ideas with the concept of the reciprocal role: a clear description of the long-established and polarised dynamics acting as the root of maladaptive patterns and behaviours (e.g. abusing to abused, contemptuous to contemptible, critical to striving).

Ryle considers that the restating of psychoanalytic ideas in cognitive terms provides a 'common language' that enables a collaborative approach to working with clients. CAT theory seeks to link early experience and the concept of reciprocal emotional roles with the 'here-and-now' interpersonal difficulties presented by clients as the immediate source of their distress and unhappiness. Psychoanalytic ideas and insights can thus be conveyed using prose descriptions and diagrams in a form of working that encourages collaboration between client and therapist and the joint exploration of meaning, including that of the evolving therapeutic relationship.

More recently, the Finnish psychologist Mikael Leiman (1992) has informed CAT theory with ideas from the Russian philosophers Lev Vygotsky and Mikhail Bakhtin, and the more widely known work of the psychoanalyst Donald Winnicott. Leiman considers that contemporary CAT theory may facilitate an integration of object relations theory and linguistics around the concept, and developmental basis, of sign-mediation. These developments have allowed CAT to move further from its roots by understanding meaning in a social, cultural and historical context as a series of ongoing dialogues mediated through the use of shared signs and symbols. This is a subtle yet important theoretical development which acknowledges the significance of the therapeutic relationship between the two unique individuals involved in the therapy: the therapist and client. Without the evolution of a shared 'language' (which can be more than words), theoretical models are likely to be employed without awareness or understanding of the client in their wider context, so reducing the benefits possible from the therapeutic relationship. Ryle has summarised the importance of this relationship as follows:

> Personality and relationships are not adequately described in terms of objects, conflicts or assumptions. They are sustained through an ongoing conversation within ourselves and with others – a conversation with roots in the past and pointing to the future. In their conversation with their patients, psychotherapists become important participants in this conversation

and, CAT, I believe, fosters the particular skills needed to find the words and other signs that patients need.

(Ryle, 2000)

In a nutshell, CAT provides an understandable and communicable integration of psychoanalytic object relations theory (with its emphasis on early development and unconscious process), with focused exploration of subjective experience in the here-and-now, using an eclectic range of tools and techniques derived from cognitive and personal construct theories. (Some background references to the sources of CAT are included at the end of this chapter as 'Further reading'.)

Theoretical model

CAT is most often used as a sixteen-session individual psychotherapy, although shorter and longer contracts are applied in some situations. It makes use of the client's capacity for self-awareness and observation of beliefs, feelings and behaviours, while acknowledging unconscious factors derived from past experience and the links between them and the therapist – client transference. CAT is an active therapy for both therapist and client. A CAT therapy has milestones which continually focus the client and therapist on the *Target Problems* (*TPs*) brought by the client, and acknowledge the time-limited nature of the work and the inevitability of termination, thus reducing the risks of excessive dependency and unrealistic expectations of the therapy.

In the early sessions much of the therapist's attention is given to understanding the client's context, history and background while asking them to describe a few TPs and to make links between past and present experience. Clients usually bring ill-defined or partially worked-through issues – such as 'uncontrollable temper', 'depression', 'loneliness', self-harm or somatic symptoms – as their TPs, and it is the therapist's task to make the links between these here-and-now problems and the client's past experience. The *Psychotherapy File* (Ryle 1990) is an ingenious psychotherapy questionnaire which is completed by the client early in the therapy and which helps as a broad screen to identify recurring patterns. What the client leaves out from their answers to the psychotherapy file is often as informative as what they put in.

By session four the therapist has to write a letter to the client, called the *Reformulation*, which is read out by the therapist in the session. In this the therapist needs to address what the client has brought to the therapy and salient historical information, and then to process the explicit TPs into Target Problem Procedures (TPPs). These explain the cyclical nature of recurrent self-defeating patterns, using the templates of *Traps, Dilemmas and Snags*.

Traps are negative feedback loops arising from false assumptions, which lead to behaviours that ultimately reinforce low self-esteem. For example, the 'Depression/Avoidance' trap: 'Feeling depressed and lacking in confidence I predict that I will not cope with social situations as others will find me uninteresting and burdensome, and reject me. I avoid going which makes me feel left out and weak for not trying. This further reinforces my lack of self-worth and makes it harder to change.'

Dilemmas are false choices or narrow options which lead to polarised ways of dealing with conflict which ultimately fail to resolve the underlying problem. For example, the 'Brute or Martyr dilemma': 'Believing that I must please others in order for them to like me, I take on more and more for others. I soon realise that my own needs are not being met and I feel resentful and taken advantage of. I then either bottle my feelings up and become the seething Martyr, or blow up and lose control (the Brute). Both result in further feelings of guilt and anger which reinforce my low self-esteem.'

Snags are more profound core beliefs which sabotage a person's success or happiness. For example the 'Safer to have nothing snag': 'Having experienced the pain of loss and abandonment it seems safer to have nothing than to risk again losing something that I love. This leaves me lonely and empty and confirms my worthlessness.'

The reformulation is a powerful tool used so early in the therapy. It ensures that the therapist has heard what the client has brought to the therapy, and it confirms that there is shared understanding of the client's life story. It is presented as a draft, and revisions are a joint responsibility. It usually has a beneficial effect on the client–therapist relationship, and boosts the therapeutic alliance if it succeeds in displaying that the therapist has listened and is beginning to make sense of the TPs. It is helpful to try to predict the likely negative transference reactions in the reformulation, and comment on these as an extension of one or more of the TPPs.

For example:

TP: 'I am unable to form any lasting, intimate relationships.'

TPP: 'Feeling unhappy and uncertain about myself it seems as if others will find me empty and unrewarding if they get beneath my skin, and will then reject me. It is therefore safer to keep a distance and reject others if they get too close. This ultimately leaves me lonely and isolated and more in need of human contact.'

Transference comment: 'Fearing rejection by anyone who really gets to know you, you may feel the need to quit the therapy earlier to try and stay in control and to avoid the risk of being hurt again. If this happens, then we need to talk about this in the sessions.'

Towards the middle of the therapy the therapist and client work towards the construction of the *Sequential Diagrammatic Reformulation (SDR)*, (a visual means of linking the TPPs with the Core State (or states)). This is where the present is firmly linked to deep-seated patterns of relating to others derived from object relations theory. CAT has developed the concept of *Reciprocal Roles* to encapsulate this: clear descriptive word pairs which crystallise the core early experiences that restrict the client to a limited repertoire of ways of relating to others. Examples of reciprocal roles are: Abandoning to Abandoned, Critical to Striving, Admiring to Admired, Abusing to Abused, Contemptuous to Contemptible. While the more powerful of the two words usually describes the behaviour of a significant adult in the client's earlier life, it is worth pointing out that no role ever exists in isolation or in just one person. From a position of trauma and devaluation (Abused, Rejected) it seems as if the only practical escape is to resort to the 'stronger' opposite (Abusing, Rejecting). Both roles are endlessly tied together in a repeating and destructive dance of action and reaction.

Clients with more profound personality disturbance are often described by using a 'split' diagram, with core reciprocal roles existing in two or more dissociated self states. This is a core feature of Ryle's CAT model of borderline personality disorder (Ryle 1997). CAT offers two template SDRs to describe two basic split-core-state constellations that have emerged from practice. In both, fantasy is used as an attempt to escape from the intolerable pain of powerless roles (see Figure 6.1). For a while it seems as if an ideal relationship has been found at last, and that all needs can now be met by reliance on the other. Nothing being perfect, disillusion or suffocation soon set in, causing a devastating feeling of anger and resentment, and the assumption of the 'strong' abuser role, which itself is unsustainable due to rejection by others and guilt about the consequences of one's abusive actions. (See Figure 6.1.)

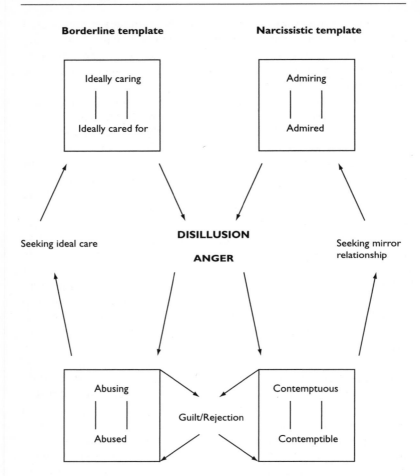

Attempts to escape from the core pain of the lower roles lead to the seeking of idealised relationships that are ultimately unsustainable.

Figure 6.1 Commonly encountered split core states.

In the second half of the therapy, client and therapist work together in a less structured way trying to recognise and revise procedures occurring in the client's life and in the therapeutic relationship. A variety of behavioural, cognitive, interpretative and creative techniques can be used to encourage insight and change via the pragmatic focusing on thoughts, feelings or actions in relation to each TPP. Most important is the development of *Exits* from the

TPPs, which are entered into the SDR and whose effectiveness is monitored using formal rating charts, recording the ability to both recognize and revise TPPs in the present. For example, for the TP 'Burn-out and stress', the TPP may be:

Fearing that I am not as good as other people I constantly try to please others and to make them like me by anticipating their needs, putting them first and working very hard to look after them. This leaves me feeling exhausted and with my needs unmet. I build up anger and resentment but am unable to express this for fear of losing control and ruining everything. This internal anger turns against me and leaves me feeling depressed and hopeless about the future.

Possible exits might be: 'Learn to say no. Express my needs assertively without losing control. Others can respect me for who I am not what I do.'

The therapy ends with the exchange of *Goodbye Letters*, a précis of the progress made, areas for further work and pitfalls for the future. Again, the exchange of written material takes on a symbolic function at the end of therapy: mutual respect, acknowledgement of the journey travelled together, acceptance of the end of the therapy and best wishes for the future. Much of the change engendered by CAT occurs beyond the last session. There is typically a follow-up session at three months to monitor progress.

CAT thus provides a formalised yet flexible structure which has the ability to engage and inspire even the more borderline and traumatised clients, by means of prose and diagrammatic demonstrations of empathic understanding and the reformulation of presented problems into overt procedures which can be challenged and modified to allow progress and change.

Older people and the CAT model

CAT is an eminently suitable model for working with older people. The early Reformulation can be hugely effective at engaging clients who are not particularly 'psychotherapy-minded' and who feel that no one will have the time to listen to and understand their life story. The highly collaborative nature of CAT helps discourage the intergenerational negative transference often encountered when working with older people who can feel 'done to' by younger 'experts' with tools and techniques beyond the comprehension of those of a less technological generation, resulting in a passive, patient powerlessness and covert anger. Older people will often find the time to work hard between the therapy sessions on diary-keeping, rating and recording the TPPs and exits, and will often see the therapy as a final chance for change and so invest tremendous energy in the tasks at hand. The developments in CAT theory derived from Vygotsky and Bakhtin are beginning to illuminate CAT practice by uncovering the importance of dialogue and meaning in a social, cultural and historical perspective. This is particularly important when working with older people whose experience and emotional language may be quite different from those of the therapist. The discovery of common ground and shared meaning can be crucial in the development of a therapeutic relationship.

Applications of cognitive analytic therapy and selection of patients

CAT, being time-limited, collaborative and generally highly communicable, is an eminently suitable psychotherapy for use with older people. One of the initial hurdles, however, is the generation of referrals in a system where the expectations of the availability and efficacy of explorative psychotherapy for older people are almost nil. Freud did not consider that older (or indeed late-middle-aged) people could benefit from psychoanalysis. This view still has a powerful influence on the thinking and practice associated with working psychodynamically with older people. Despite notable challenges to Freud's ageist assumptions as early as 1919 (Abraham 1919), the association between the concepts 'older' and 'too late' thrives. Even when conscious prejudice has faded away, the lingering unconscious barriers to working with older people are reflected in the continuing paucity of practitioners who actually do psychotherapy with older people. In a lecture in 1989, Hildebrand stated:

> Psychoanalysis can make a major contribution to our understanding of the dynamics of later life ... no other theory can account for feelings of abandonment and despair, intimacy and isolation, arrogance and disdain, stagnation and creativity as each of us struggles with the developmental task of 'the third age'.

CAT can enable psychodynamic understanding of age-specific

stresses in a way that is both highly acceptable to and practical for older people. Furthermore, for the large numbers of older people in contact with mental health services who, by reason of cognitive impairment or involutional despair, are unable to engage in individual work, CAT insights can open doors of understanding and self-reflection in professionals and carers – which in turn benefits the older people themselves, who are battling with the most severe of threats to their ego integrity and humanity. The use of CAT in this wider context (systemic CAT) is an exciting development. Selection of older people for CAT, therefore, must take into account these two modalities.

Selection of patients for individual CAT (see Figure 6.2)

Older people are more likely than younger people to have some form of disability. Disability generally cannot be seen as a hindrance to receiving psychotherapy. The task of the practitioner is to *enable* the older person to partake as fully as possible. Although sometimes complex and challenging hurdles appear, it should go without saying that access to buildings, aids to hearing and vision and acceptable transport services should be made available to older people routinely. CAT has the flexibility to present material and engage the older person using verbal dialogue, prose writing, and diagrammatic and nonverbal techniques, allowing adaptation to sensory impairment or language difficulty.

The ability to engage in CAT is the one crucial criterion in selection of patients. It is quite permissible to offer a series of assessment sessions to explore the ability of a person to engage prior to starting the CAT proper. While a certain amount of flexibility is needed to accommodate the greater number of reality-based hurdles older people have to face (for example, delayed transport, periods of physical illness during the therapy, clashing hospital appointments, etc.), there is still a need to maintain the boundaries of the therapy firmly when possible, or at least adapt them to novel situations with thought and consideration.

CAT has developed a reputation for being an effective and manageable way of offering help to people with 'personality disorder' or, more particularly, the more self-damaging and fragmented personality structures resulting from traumatic and abusive experience – the concept of 'borderline traits'. In the context of a health service that faces the necessity of rationing services on the basis of need and severity of need, it would seem logical to offer CAT to this group preferentially; their distress and use of services are high, and the opportunities for change are substantial when there is clearly traumatic experience available to be understood and worked through. The concept of 'personality disorder' in later life is little researched or discussed, perhaps largely due to the fact that, as a construction, it is flawed in relation to older people. Traditionally in psychiatry textbooks there are references to personality disorder 'burning out' in mid-life, and an assumption that the prevalence of personality disorder tapers away by retirement age due to either a diminution in the intensity of traumatic memories with time, or an increase in suicide in this group.

It is the experience of many of those working with older people that this assumption is simply not true – a position now supported by some research evidence (Reich *et al.* 1988). It is not uncommon for older people to disclose childhood sexual abuse for the first time in their eighties or older. Freud regarded the unconscious as 'timeless' and experience suggests that memories of trauma seventy years old can be highly vivid and disabling. Moreover, there is a small but growing body of work suggesting that borderline traits are often quiescent in middle age, only to experience a resurgence in later life as cumulative life events and insults to an individual's adaptability and coping repertoire compound each other (Hepple 1999, Morse and Lynch 2000). Later life is thus the time when the distress and related self-destructive behaviours present to services. It is surely the best time, therefore, to offer treatment.

Narcissism, as understood by CAT, is a more covert variant of the borderline concept. Where physical and sexual abuse can lead to a typical borderline pathology, emotional deprivation and highly critical care as a child can generate the belief that perfection is the only acceptable outcome in relation to the self and others (see Figure 6.1). Where self-esteem is integrally related to the effect that looks, or physical or mental abilities have on admiring others, increasing age can make the fantasy harder and harder to sustain. The concept of narcissistic collapse in later life explains how often highly successful people find that the losses of later life prevent them from sustaining the admiring to admired fantasy, causing a devastating fall in self-esteem, a feeling of resentment and rejection, and the journey into self-neglect, pseudo-dementia or more overt self-harm.

Older people with personality-based problems can present with a myriad of symptoms. Professionals often identify the need for a developmental formulation of the person's situation by the use of diagnostic comments such as 'difficult personality' or 'personality factors' or even 'highly manipulative'. Common symptom clusters include 'treatment-resistant' or chronic 'low-grade' depressions, multiple somatic symptoms and sick-role behaviours, hysterical pseudo-dementia, self-neglect and withdrawal, abuse of alcohol and drugs (particularly prescribed medications), and angry rejection and social isolation based on a fear of intimacy, in addition to the more overt borderline spectrum problems described in DSM-IV.

CAT could be seen as the treatment of choice for older people with 'personality difficulties' (see Figure 6.2). The core link to be made in individual therapy is between recent losses (job, partner, mobility) and past trauma or abuse. These patients have often experienced years of loose contact with services and have dabbled with multiple drug treatments and supportive psychological and social care strategies, with little benefit. This group is, perhaps, the bread-and-butter clientele for a CAT therapist working with older people. They have chronic and often severe distress with traumatic antecedents and a lifetime of perpetuation of negatively reinforcing beliefs and behaviours. They are unlikely to be helped by non-psychodynamic approaches and so the cost-effectiveness of CAT becomes a paramount factor in its choice in public sector services.

For example, an 82-year-old woman recently admitted to a nursing home with failing physical health cuts her wrists with a broken glass as a suicide attempt. Further disturbed behaviour, resistiveness to care, verbal abuse of staff and pseudo-seizures alert the team to underlying personality disturbance, and a history of childhood sexual abuse is uncovered at a case conference. Depressive symptoms are monitored by the psychiatric team but the mainstay of treatment is individual CAT. Similarly, a 58-year-old man presents to a memory clinic with a twelve-year history of memory problems which are functionally very disabling and prevent meaningful communication between the man and his wife. Cognitive testing reveals an inconsistent picture not typical of organic dysfunction, and investigations are normal. Over time the hypothesis is built up that there must be an underlying psychological problem and that the man is 'cutting off' from the real distress. The symptoms began following early retirement from a responsible job in the armed forces due to stress and burn-out. A history of a physically abusive father who demanded perfection in terms of career and attainment, and a mother who 'cut off' through drink, drugs and latterly real dementia, provides the historical links to form the basis of a CAT reformulation. The client is offered individual CAT.

As with younger people, the therapist must resist the temptation to explore the antecedents in depth while the crisis is acute, although the pressures to 'offer something' may be great, due to the often uncomfortable countertransference engendered in those working with older people with severe self-destructive behaviours. The author would not attempt individual CAT with an acute in-patient, although CAT insights can greatly enable a staff group split by severe borderline dynamics, when used systemically.

All this focus on more severe personality disturbance should not detract from CAT's ability to help those with less profound problems. Acute depression, bereavement, adjustment disorders and anxiety-based disorders have been, and will continue to be, treated by CAT successfully. As an eclectic therapy, CAT can call on techniques from cognitive or behaviour therapy (such as graded exposure and the challenging of negative automatic thoughts), while having the depth to dig deeper as needed.

Selection of patients for systemic CAT

Insights gained by applying the CAT model can prove helpful in cases where a person is unable to engage in meaningful individual work, due either to the severity of their distress or the presence of greater than mild cognitive impairment. CAT can provide a comprehensible framework, for all those involved in the wider system around an identified patient, to provide insight into feelings and

Figure 6.2 Selection of older patients for individual CAT

Trend to suitability	*Trend to unsuitability*
• Stable 'personality disorder' with traumatic or abusive antecedents (common derogatory labels: 'highly manipulative', 'behavioural', etc.)	• Patients in acute crisis or acute in-patients
	• Acute psychosis or delirium
• Somatisation syndromes resistant to CBT	• Significant cognitive impairment (particularly short-term memory deficits)
• Atypical and treatment-resistant depression	
• Hysterical pseudo-dementia, pseudo-seizures and self-neglect syndromes	

emotional reactions generated by the system, to work out how individuals are involved in perpetuating problematic procedures, and to formulate *System Exits*. The formulation of a *System SDR* at a case conference setting can be a surprisingly easy way to use CAT as a tool for consultation and support of professionals and carers, thus reducing the level of distress and limiting the damage caused by destructive or violent behaviours.

Figure 6.3 demonstrates a system SDR worked out over a number of case conferences involving over a dozen different people, including doctors, community mental health team workers, home-care staff, relatives, voluntary sector staff and the identified patient. The patient in this case is a woman in her seventies who had experienced a resurgence of borderline traits following the death of her disabled husband. She had had childhood experience of polio and had experienced the criticism of her family for the cost of her treatment (pre-National Health Service) and the effect of this on the other siblings. It seems as if the only care she received was from hospital staff during lengthy in-patient stays, which provided the antecedents for a conversion of her distress into somatic symptoms. Her marriage provided the opportunity for her to enact an ideally caring role with her husband, which contained her symptoms. Following his death, the system around her was thrown into turmoil due to repeated self-harm, threats of litigation and national 'hospital shopping' (seeking multiple second opinions in different parts of the country).

All those involved in the case have, at times, experienced abusive rejection alternating with idealisation. To the unwary, the powerful dynamics at work created opportunities for re-enactment of polarised reciprocal roles, which caused significant splits amongst the professionals and carers involved. Idealisation of a new doctor or expert introduced to the system, for example, generated devaluation of existing carers and professionals. As each 'honeymoon' period ended with disillusion and abusive rage, those involved were subjected to further uncomfortable projections, with the temptation to engage in rejection and ridicule of the identified patient, as abusive reciprocal roles were again enacted. This usually resulted in further self-harm, leaving professionals and carers feeling helpless, guilty and 'burnt out'. So challenging were the dynamics involved that the health of many in the system was at significant risk.

By use of the systemic CAT model, feelings could be described

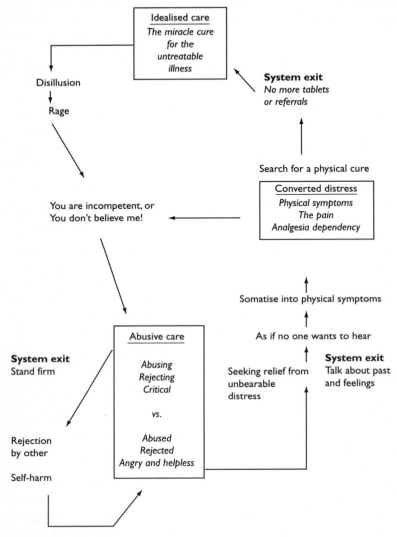

Figure 6.3 Systemic SDR for an older patient with severe borderline personality traits.

and contained, system exits could be formulated and a sense of working together and mutual support engendered. As time has passed, relative stability has been achieved and the potential damage has been limited. The patient is still unable to engage in individual work. She is, however, invited to the case conferences and receives the full minutes and current SDR, even if she is unable to attend.

Another potential area for the application of the systemic CAT model is that of dementia care. Although the identified patients are often unable to engage in individual work, the reciprocal roles generated by work with confused and highly dependent older people are often powerful, regressive and responsible for 'innocent' infantalisation or more overt elder abuse. Describing and processing these roles is likely to be highly beneficial to professionals, carers and the older people themselves. Recently, Dr Laura Sutton has restated Tom Kitwood's social psychology understanding of transference relationships in dementia care, using the reciprocal role model (Sutton, in press). The development of a vocabulary to begin a dialogue in this field has opened the door to use of systemic CAT in a little-charted territory. Figure 6.4 illustrates some of Dr Sutton's ideas.

Walter Wills and Bob Woods (1997) have begun some work on describing the nature of the relationship between professional (Admiral nurses) and informal carers of people with dementia living in their homes, using techniques from personal construct theory and ideas developed from CAT. In particular they identify the prevalence of the 'Placation Trap' in the relationship between the Admiral nurse and the informal carer, and suggest that it serves as a tool for avoiding conflict and hinders the processing of powerful feelings generated from work with those with dementia.

Figure 6.4 Reciprocal roles in dementia care

Malignant	*Supportive*
Infantilising – infantilised	Negotiating – safely involved
Depersonalising – depersonalised	Contacting – connected
Ridiculing – humiliated	Holding – enabled

Therapy in practice

In order to give a flavour of individual CAT with an older client it seems natural to use a single, detailed case discussion. There seems at least as much to be gained from detailed analysis of a single case as from generalisations about many.

As the therapist in this case was the author, 'I' has been used to refer to the therapist throughout. 'Mr Smith' is not the client's real name and permission to use this case material has been obtained. Mr Smith kept a regular diary of his thoughts and feelings as the therapy progressed, and completed the Psychotherapy File prior to the first session.

Case illustration and discussion: Mr Smith
Therapist: Jason Hepple

History

Mr Smith was a 66-year-old retired merchant seaman. The over-whelming influence in his early development and indeed his whole life was his mother, whom he usually called, somewhat sarcastically, 'Lady Bountiful'. Born midway between the two world wars, both he and his father – a shy and retiring aircraft engineer, appear to have been completely dominated by a woman who was extremely controlling and intolerant of the needs and feelings of her family. She labelled them as 'ungrateful' and 'self-ish', while striving herself to maintain the high standards witnessed by the outside world. She communicated clearly with Mr Smith that he was unwanted, and Mr Smith suspected that she really desired a daughter. She was always withholding of love and often extremely cruel. For example, when he was 7 she made him kill a kitten he had found, with an iron bar, as he 'didn't deserve a pet'. These incidents left Mr Smith feeling guilty that he was not pleasing his mother and determined to try harder to win her affection.

When Mr Smith was 16 he left home and joined the merchant navy. It was while he was away that his mother had the daughter she had so longed for, 'Dee', for whom nothing was too much trouble. Mr Smith recounts a tremendous sense of injustice that Dee was freely given all the things he had wanted so badly. After a spell in the RAF, Mr Smith continued a career in the merchant navy, always supporting his parents and sister financially, buying a house for them and living with them when not away on duty. During the therapy, he was still in a relationship of forty years' duration with a lady he called by her initials, but he had never been able to develop this beyond visiting her one or two nights a week, for fear of letting his mother down. He thus never separated from his parents, and it was not until he was in his sixties, ten years after his father's death, that the mother he had spent his life trying to please decided to go and live with her daughter and 'model' family in the South East, on the pretext that she could put up with Mr Smith no longer. It was then that his brother-in-law started legal proceedings to gain ownership of Mr Smith's house, saying that it *de facto* belonged to his mother, despite Mr Smith having paid every penny of the mortgage. It was during this period that Mr Smith developed depression and vague unexplained physical symptoms which he called 'my condition', which failed to respond to psychiatric treatments including ECT.

Phase of assessment (sessions one to five)

Mr Smith appeared early for his first appointment and presented as an imposing figure: tall, large, young for his age, a conspicuous walking stick and several layers of old and worn jumpers and cardigans, topped with a slightly too small duffle coat. He appeared both mildly eccentric and also vaguely intimidating. Despite this, he was very respectful of me and seemed committed to the treatment, treating me as a young officer who, by virtue of status rather than experience, would know the correct way forward. The Target Problems fell into two main areas.

> **My condition** – a vague collection of fluctuating head and back pains which caused a retreat to his bed, sometimes for days on end.

> **Blowing up** – an admission to sudden outbursts of rage and frustration when he felt that people were taking him for granted. This second problem was well exemplified by Mr Smith's relationship with a disabled lady in her nineties for whom he did jobs, and who tirelessly took advantage of his good nature, resulting in abrupt and angry departures from her flat without Mr Smith being able to express his feelings to her

or negotiate any boundaries with her. If he did not go back and apologise, he felt himself to be spoilt and ungrateful.

The taking of the history and unravelling of these problems was a laborious exercise, as factual accounts were often interspersed with minor political tirades against the youth of the day and the selfishness of 1990s society. These reflections helped me, in supervision, to identify part of the negative transference: the desire to please me, due to my status, but covert contempt for me as a representative of a world that had left Mr Smith behind in its evolution towards the rights of self over the concept of community.

Mr Smith's completion of the psychotherapy file displayed his domination by intense emotional states which seemed unamenable to logical reason, and also his meticulous need for documentation in an attempt to ensure that he was properly understood. His diary-keeping involved pages of handwritten reflections on the week's events, written on government notepaper. Simply going through the diary could consume a whole session and often resulted in us failing to see the wood for the density of the trees. My addition of strict agenda-setting at the start of each session helped with this. It was not until session five that I felt able to compose the reformulation.

Reformulation: I was keen to reassure Mr Smith that he had been heard and to identify the pain involved in digging up memories that had been repressed or defended against for up to six decades.

Reformulation letter

> *Dear Mr Smith*
> *Now that we have had five sessions of our cognitive analytic therapy, I would like to present you with this reformulation. I will try to summarise what I see as the main themes that have emerged from our discussions, which will help us to focus on some of the important issues during the remaining eleven sessions. I would like you to see this as a draft; we will be able to work on this together in the next few sessions, and any changes you would like to make can be added.*
> *I have been very impressed by your enthusiasm for the therapy, and the work you have put in between sessions. I realise*

how difficult it is to start digging up painful memories from the past, especially after so many years. I think the sessions we have had so far have been very useful and I am looking forward to moving forward with you.

You have suffered from nagging physical symptoms and feelings of depression and hopelessness for many years. It seems as if you have been ill for as long as you can remember. In the past these have been treated as an illness with various drugs and ECT. The approach we are taking is at last trying to understand these feelings in the context of the experiences you have had in your life; attempting to ask the question 'why', maybe for the first time.

We have talked about many painful experiences from your past, especially your childhood. Your mother has been a very powerful influence on you throughout your life, even to this day. The overwhelming experience seems to have been that you always felt unwanted by your mother. Despite saying that she loved you, she always seemed to have plenty to give to other people, especially your sister Dee, but never anything for you. 'Lady Bountiful', as you call her, gave your bed away when you were twelve. You never seemed to be able to live up to her high and exacting standards; never able to please her. Everything you did was inferior when compared to others. She told you that you were not good enough for her and that you were a disgrace. She couldn't even allow you to have anything special for yourself. You badly wanted to have a pet to love, but this was forbidden. When you found some kittens she made you beat them to death. When you managed to keep a mouse, 'Charlie', she threatened to kill it and eventually gassed it in front of you.

If you ever dared to feel resentful or unjustly treated you were told you were jealous and ungrateful. It has never been possible to be angry with your mother for the cruel things that she did to you. You have ended up blaming yourself and keeping all the frustration inside, while trying to think the best of your mother. After a lifetime of trying to please her and win her approval, even buying a house for her and your father to live in, she has now turned her back on you completely and is still trying to take things away from you. This must be very painful.

I would like to summarise the main problems as follows:

Target Problem: 'My condition'

1 **The 'safer to have nothing' snag:** *It seems as if you can never have anything for yourself. It feels as if you don't deserve anything, and that anything you do have is likely to be taken away or destroyed in front of you. The only things you can have are things other people don't want, like the discarded wood and pencils you collect. Despite being in a relationship for nearly forty years, you have never felt able to get married – it seemed safer to stay at a distance for fear of losing everything if you accepted something for yourself.*

Target Problem: 'Blowing up'

2 **The placation trap:** *Being uncertain about your own self-worth, you have always tried to please other people for fear of upsetting them. By doing this you are likely to be taken advantage of, leaving you feeling angry and frustrated and ultimately guilty about having these feelings.*

3 **The 'Brute' or 'Martyr' dilemma:** *Either you put up with things silently, feeling resentful (the Martyr – physical symptoms), or you 'blow up' and finally lose your temper (the Brute). As you put it, if you don't stand up for yourself, others will see you as a 'mug'.*

We shall start to work on these problems in the next few sessions. We must watch out for some of these things happening in the therapy; it will be tempting to please me and keep negative or angry feelings to yourself, for fear of damaging the therapy. It will be better to talk about them in the therapy rather than dwell on them later.

I look forward to the rest of our work together.

Working towards an SDR (sessions six to nine)

The reformulation was rather too easily accepted, which I suspected was partly a dismissive reaction and an unwillingness to show the covert anger that was clearly under the surface, at this stage. To focus in more clearly, we began to work on the TPPs individually on separate sheets. Progress was slow in coming – the continuing legal wrangling over the house preoccupied the diaries and distracted from the TPPs. For simplicity, TPPs 2 and 3 were combined at this stage, linking the placation trap with the dilemma. While Mr Smith accepted the arguments I presented, I was constantly left with the feeling of being partly humoured – if he put up with my agenda items, he could spend twenty minutes attempting to gain my approval for the latest developments in his legal action.

Mr Smith began to communicate more of his feelings to me in his dreams. In session seven he told me how he had dreamt of a head-line describing how he had beaten his mother to death and how I was blamed for this as his psychiatrist. In the next session, a doctor in a white coat was mangled by a huge mechanical thing with long silver tentacles (which for Mr Smith represented his mother). I was symbolically taking on his rage towards his mother – transferred as disappointment towards me in that I was unable to offer an ideal solution to his distress – and he seemed concerned that I would not survive the confrontation. In session nine, I interpreted this rage explicitly, and his fear that his feelings would destroy both of us if he showed them to me, and that I was unable to 'order' him how to change for the better. He became very upset and tearful in this session, and it seemed we had made a small breakthrough. In session ten we began to work together on the SDR – I was keen to encourage collaboration rather than present him with another detailed document he could politely ignore or refute with reams of testimony.

SDR

This formed clearly in session ten. We had already identified the core reciprocal roles in our attempts to lay out the condensed TPPs. We identified the internal parent as withholding, contemptuous, abusing and controlling, and the child as striving, contemptible, abused and controlled, but with hidden rage and destructiveness. The split-off ideal state (admiring and admired) represented the possibility of resolution of the unrequited need for love and care by a repetition compulsion of the tireless need to placate. The dilemma is represented by two ways of dealing with the rage and resentment generated by the frustration of the ideal, i.e. dangerous explosions or repressed and somatised angry feelings. The failure in self-care snag leads to an unstable but safe position of control and cut-off contempt for the world.

The structure is essentially the narcissistic pattern and while these visual representations of his core pain seemed more digestible than the prose reformulation, the addition of exits was much resisted and we often spent much time confirming the accuracy of the SDR rather than working on the exits.

Both SDRs are really a single loop which eventually ends where it began, in the powerless child part of the reciprocal roles: contemptible/abused or striving/inadequate/helpless. Start at these points (* in Figures 6.5 and 6.6) to begin tracing the pattern following the arrows. Exits are points for potential therapeutic intervention.

Active therapy (sessions ten to fourteen)

While we had addressed the hidden rage and resentment, there still seemed great difficulty in moving away from a more and more detailed description of the past, towards ways of enabling change in the future. I attempted to interpret this with reference to TPP 1 – 'safer to have nothing' – especially in relation to a therapy that was going to end, and also identified the tremendous grief involved in acknowledging the decades spent in nurturing these self-destructive patterns of behaviour. It is always the case that exits must come from the client, and eventually three simple exits emerged: 'Spoil myself a little bit', 'I can only do so much. Express my own needs'

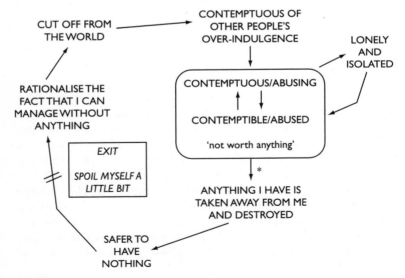

Figure 6.5 SDR I – the 'safer to have nothing' snag.

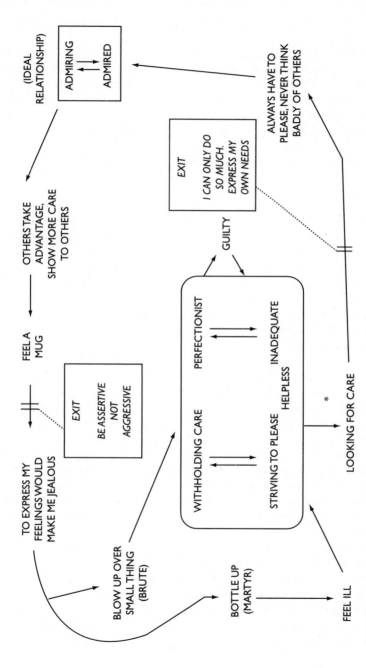

Figure 6.6 'I must always please others'.

and 'Be assertive not aggressive.' We were beginning to move forward.

I feel that Mr Smith's age made it particularly difficult to move on from the past – to do so at this stage represented something of a defeat and a feeling that his mother had somehow won (or the giving up of the ideal that his mother was really loving towards him and would one day see the error of her ways and acknowledge all Mr Smith had done for her). Change came in the form of Mr Smith concluding the legal settlement of the house issue, and in session thirteen he managed to open some of his Christmas presents and started to talk of planning a holiday for himself.

Ending (sessions fourteen and fifteen)

One could anticipate from Mr Smith's history that endings might seem unreal or might in some way be only temporary, as his experience of loss was limited, his mother still being alive at 93; apart from his father, he had suffered no other significant bereavements. It was going to be important to underline the concreteness of the ending while offering the insights he had gained as gifts he could have for himself if he chose, to make his life better for himself.

Mr Smith claimed that he was too ill to attend session fourteen so I offered a replacement the following week. I felt that this represented both a denial of the termination and his ambivalence towards daring to change with so few sessions left, and this was exemplified further by Mr Smith saying that he had planned a weekend away but was again too ill to go, and that he had gone out to buy a much-needed replacement toothbrush, but had been overwhelmed by the choice and had returned empty-handed. I pointed out the closeness of the ending and the need to begin taking the responsibility for change on himself, and that by his actions he had shown he knew what he might do to 'spoil himself', and that this was progress. He would be able to do it without me.

Session fifteen saw Mr Smith sporting a new haircut and a renewed enthusiasm to understand the SDR and take away the tools necessary for change. We concentrated on the exits, especially the ability to be assertive while feeling in control of the aggressive and out-of-control feelings that confrontation brought up. We role-played setting boundaries with the elderly lady Mr Smith had taken under his wing. I read out the goodbye letter and invited him to reply in the last session. He became very tearful as I read the letter, but seemed more comfortable in showing me some of his pain overtly.

Goodbye letters

In my letter to Mr Smith I was keen to point out that I saw the sixteen sessions as just the beginning and that he had gained the insights to progress with the exits we had planned together. I identified his likely feeling of abandonment, especially as a repeat of his previous experience of physical psychiatric treatments – being discharged at the end of his course of ECT feeling no better and without offers of further help or treatment. I described the two contracted TPPs and their exits in some detail to further emphasise them. I also explicitly described the young officer transference and the anger with me when he realised I could not give the orders necessary for his cure, and that the responsibility for change rested mainly with him.

In Mr Smith's long, handwritten goodbye letter to me, I was pleased with the degree of self-reflection he now seemed capable of. He talked coherently about the exits and his difficulty turning thought into action, and wrote in large letters: 'Go back to SDR. Read and think it out!' There was an element of placation in the general tone – a desire to leave me feeling that he had made progress, which we addressed to some extent.

Goodbye letter to Mr Smith

Dear Mr Smith
Now that we have reached the end of our therapy, I would like to give you this letter. It is to say goodbye and to put in writing how I see the progress we have made in our sixteen sessions working together.

When we first met, you had been feeling unwell for many years. You described this as your 'condition'. You told me about the feelings of hopelessness, depression, feeling isolated and cut off from the world, the many physical symptoms that made you take to your bed for long periods and the irritability you felt towards the people who are close to you. Despite seeing many specialists you were left feeling that no one could help you. Even after you were treated in the hospital for a period of depression, you left feeling abandoned and unwanted. No one seemed to care.

We started with the idea that how you are in the present is a reflection of your experiences in the past. We have discovered how many of the feelings you describe are rooted in your childhood, especially your relationship with your mother. She seemed to value everyone else over you. She was 'Lady Bountiful' in other people's eyes, but to you she was cruel and demanding of more than you could ever give. She destroyed all the things that you loved most. If you ever complained you were ungrateful and jealous. In your attempts to please her and eventually win her love, you gave over a large part of your life in caring for and supporting your parents, always at the expense of your own needs. Even this was not enough and she has now deserted you and devalues all you have done for her.

It is from this experience that we derived your target problem procedures which gradually grew into the SDRs that we have been working on in the second half of our therapy. They ended up as two core beliefs:

1 Safer to have nothing: 'It is safer to have nothing than risk having something I love taken away and destroyed. I can do without things. People who want things are wasteful and selfish.' This pattern leaves you empty and isolated, with nothing to look forward to in life. You have found it very difficult to accept anything for yourself during therapy, although you have become good at identifying this problem; even going so far as thinking how you might 'treat yourself a bit'. The next step is to put this awareness into action. I think you are nearly at this point.

2 I must always please others: 'If I do enough for them, they will eventually treat me with respect and anticipate my needs. I must put them first.' This pattern always leads to you feeling taken advantage of, being made 'a mug'. This is when all the sadness and resentment starts to well up as anger inside you. You then either 'blow up' and become the 'brute' or bottle it all up again, take to your bed with illness and feel the 'martyr'. Still your needs are not met. Guilt starts you off on this cycle again. In therapy you have become aware of this pattern in your close relationships. It happens time and time again with your partner and you are acutely aware of the similarity of this relationship *to that between you and your mother. The exit from this pattern is to express your needs, to tell people you can only do so much and to tread the fine line between being assertive and being aggressive. I think you are doing well with this and are already putting your insight into action. This is the beginning.*

Some of these patterns have appeared in our relationship in the therapy. At first I think you saw me as a young commanding officer who would solve your problems by taking control from you. You just had to obey orders, please me and I would tell you the answers. When you realised I could not do this, and that the answers had to come from within you, you felt duped by me, and angry with me for leading you on in this way. You had fantasies of shooting me at this time. I had let you down. Gradually you began to trust me in a new way and we began to work together on your problems. I think you began to know that I respect you for who you really are and not for what you do for me.

After our last session, you will probably feel let down and abandoned again. This may make it difficult to accept for yourself the many positive things you have to take away from the therapy. The end of the therapy is the point we have been working towards. I am giving your therapy to you. I know you can take it and use it to make your life better for yourself. Please accept it.

Finally may I thank you for the great deal of energy and commitment you have shown to me and your therapy. I know how hard it has been at times but your strength and determination have seen you through to the end. My thoughts will be with you in the future.

Bon Voyage!

Goodbye letter from Mr Smith to JH

Thank you very much for all your help, patience, understanding and professionalism.

What a long and painful road it has been. To give a small insight of the length and distance travelled; may I recall a day in August 1994.

I was leaving the [hospital] after a 'foggy' session with Dr X, she having arranged for me to see you. I said to myself, mother is not going to be discussed. I suppose it was too painful for me to think about. I _was_ to blame: it was all my fault. She _was_ on my mind like a heavy weight. A burden of incalculable confusion and unhappiness.

I feel my life has been wasted, I could have done more, become more, and given more. I do not feel as much hostility to mother as before but have I got to be angry and 'mad' to be entirely free of her pernicious influence?

At the moment the emphasis is upon trying to clear-up all the things which have been forgotten, avoided, or neglected. What a sad waste of time it has all been.

I'm not satisfied with my little progress at 'spoiling' myself. I must work harder at this and think about it more often. I find it difficult to see myself as I really am. However, I used a tin of shaving foam which has been in my possession for a long time. Instead of using face-soap as usual. 'Such indulgences could be construed as conspicuous consumption!!!'

On Thursday I passed a waste skip in the road and I had to take some wood for [my partner's] fire. This is totally irrational. I have enough wood to last a lifetime. On the other hand I'm under pressure to 'slim-down' my belongings, and here I am collecting more. 'It is such a shame to waste!!' 'Go back to SDR. Read and think it out!'

Why haven't I the motivation to go on holiday? My dear old car needs reparations first. Is the weather too inclement? Have I lost the art of living, and like a worker just toil away at what needs to be done? Am I just weary of the struggle and just too unwell to 'get up and go'? Am I too blasé about what the world holds for me? Is it mother's puritanical example; is she telling me in my sub-conscious; there are too many things to be done, I have been negligent and neglectful, things need to be attended to. I'm a disgrace and the situation must be remedied. At least I am trying to see and question.

I must not overburden myself with all the many things I have to do. I must do what I can, and then say I have done so much and I must relax and indulge myself a little.

Thank you again for your great help. It has been indispensable to me. I was a 'no hoper'. I will do my best to remember what you have taught me and constantly consider and re-appraise.

I will try to repay what has been invested in me. By helping

*my fellow creatures all I can and be kind and understanding to
the less fortunate.*

*I will miss our sessions; but I will do my best to apply all that
you have so unstintingly taught me.*

Mr Smith

The last session

The mood was very optimistic and positive, and Mr Smith read his
goodbye letter to me. I was left with the feeling that things were
going a bit too well, but decided against rocking the boat at this
stage.

Rating charts

Two charts were used and both followed a similar pattern for both
recognition and revision, with stasis until session eight and then
steady progress. Enacting 'spoiling myself a bit' was rated as actually worsening in the last third of the therapy – a recognition of the
ambivalence towards risking change when the ending loomed.

Follow-up

Our meeting after three months had the air of a happy military
reunion to enjoy the reliving of past trials and update on more
recent events. He was keen to tell me about the exits he had
achieved – going on holiday, putting his house on the market to
move to a newer and less draughty flat with fewer memories, and
buying himself new clothes – but was also determined to point out
that things were still hard and that small changes were still difficult
to enact. Physical symptoms were not mentioned. We parted easily
and positively and no further follow-up was planned.

Transference and countertransference

I have discussed the transference during the course of recounting the
sessional material. The main aspect was 'the young officer' with its
elements of respect and idealised expectation countered by hidden
distrust and ridicule at my youth and lack of experience. I feel we
addressed this well in the second half of the therapy and developed a
more adult-to-adult relationship, as exemplified in the follow-up.

Supervision helped me work with the countertransference: the temptation to tell him what to do and prove my expertise by coming up with complex written solutions which he could secretly dismiss. Constantly trying to maintain a collaborative approach and deal with feeling issues that arose helped with this. I was also supported by my supervision group in containing the murderous rage and covert communication of violent feelings towards me.

I learned a great deal from Mr Smith, notably the need to be patient and persistent with older patients and to be aware of the culture of low expectations and difficulty in countenancing change in problems that have existed for longer than I have lived. The SDR proved the most useful tool for Mr Smith – visual images seemed to make more contact with his unconscious material, when he had for so long defended against it with detailed letters and notes to himself in a complex and idiosyncratic prose style. I was pleased that my failure to focus on Mr Smith's physical symptoms, probably due to intimidation rather than design, proved to be successful in their dispersal. In terms of my mistakes, in retrospect, I would have taken more control of the course of the sessions by clear agenda-setting straight away, and would have addressed the covert rage towards me at an earlier stage. Overall, I feel the CAT was a positive experience for both of us and I am left with fond memories and great respect for a man brave enough to try and change at this stage in his life.

Summary

Cognitive analytic therapy seems well suited to working with older people. It offers a structured, time-limited and psychodynamically-based intervention which can benefit those with depression and anxiety-based disorders with antecedents in earlier life experiences, as well as the more 'difficult' or 'treatment resistant' patients with borderline personality traits or tendencies towards somatisation, conversion and dissociation.

CAT, by the discovery of shared meaning and understanding, is a collaborative exploration of the other's life and experience. It has both the depth and flexibility to be an effective way of working psychotherapeutically with older people.

Further reading

ACAT online. *http://www.acat.org.uk*

Beck, A.T. (1976). *Cognitive Therapy and the Emotional Disorders*. New York: International Universities Press.

Kelly, G.A. (1955). *The Psychology of Personal Constructs*. New York: Norton.

Malan, D. (1979). *Individual Psychotherapy and the Science of Psychodynamics*. London: Butterworth.

Ryle, A. (1997). *Cognitive Analytic Therapy and Borderline Personality Disorder. The Model and the Method*. Chichester. John Wiley & Sons.

References

Abraham, K. (1919). The applicability of psychoanalytic treatment to patients of an advanced age. In: *Selected Papers on Psychoanalysis*. London: Hogarth Press.

Hepple, J. (1999). Borderline traits and dissociated states in later life. Insights from Cognitive Analytic Therapy. *PSIGE Newsletter*, 70, 20–23.

Hildebrand, H.P. (1989). Towards an understanding of the dynamics of later life. *Proceedings of the Third International Psychogeriatric Congress*, Chicago, 1987.

Leiman, M. (1992). The concept of sign in the work of Vygotsky, Winnicott and Bakhtin: Further integration of object relations theory and activity theory. *British Journal of Medical Psychology*, 65, 209–221.

Morse, J.Q. and Lynch, T.R. (2000). Personality disorders in late life. *Current Psychiatry Reports*, 2, 24–31.

Reich, J., Nduaguba, M. and Yates, W. (1988). Age and sex distribution of DSM-III personality cluster traits in a community population. *Comprehensive Psychiatry*, 29(3), 298–303.

Ryle, A. (1990). *Cognitive Analytic Therapy: Active Participation in Change. A New Integration in Brief Psychotherapy*. Chichester: Wiley.

Ryle, A. (1997). The structure and development of borderline personality disorder: A proposed model. *British Journal of Psychiatry*, 170, 82–87.

Ryle, A. (2000). What theory is CAT based on? Origins of CAT. ACAT online. http://www.acat.org.uk (5 October 2000).

Ryle, A. and Golynkina, K. (2000). Effectiveness of time-limited cognitive analytic therapy of borderline personality disorder: factors associated with outcome. *British Journal of Medical Psychology*, 73, 197–210.

Sutton, L. (in press). When late life brings a diagnosis of Alzheimer's Disease and early life brought trauma. A cognitive-analytic understanding of loss of mind. *Journal of Clinical Psychology and Psychotherapy*.

Wills, W. and Woods, B. (1997). Developing a specialist nursing service for family care-givers of people with dementia: dilemmas of role expectation, perceived dependency and control. In: P. Denicolo and M. Pope (eds) *Sharing and Understanding Practice*. European Personal Construct Association, 241–255.

Chapter 7

Psychological therapies with older people

An overview

Jason Hepple, Philip Wilkinson and Jane Pearce

Faced with a range of therapies that promise benefits to older people, the busy clinician will need to know how best to choose a therapy that may suit a given patient. This will involve an awareness of the therapies available, some knowledge of their effectiveness with older people, and an ability to match therapy to patient and patient to therapy. The clinician may also have a wider interest in promoting and developing psychological treatment services for older patients.

Ageism in service provision?

> Near or above the age of fifty the elasticity of mental processes, on which the treatment depends, is as a rule lacking – old people are no longer educable.
>
> (Freud 1905)

Despite optimism that things have moved on from Freud's bleak view of the value of psychotherapy for older people, Siobhan Murphy's survey of one hundred UK psychotherapy departments demonstrates that, nearly one hundred years later, psychotherapy for older people is often a scarce resource (Murphy 2000). Eighty-seven per cent of respondents felt that their services failed to deliver to older people compared to services for a younger age group in their catchment area. The respondents drew attention to the lack of referrals of older people to psychotherapy services; the over-75 age group represented less than 1 per cent of referrals despite forming over 8 per cent of the population. Most striking in this survey was the low rate of referral of the over-55s by old age physicians and old age psychiatrists, compared to referrals from their colleagues in general adult psychiatry.

Different reasons for low referral rates have been suggested, such as 'professional ageism', but this may be oversimplifying the problem.

> Ageism on the part of professionals has not yet been demonstrated to account for insufficient mental health services to the aged. Instead, systemic factors, such as accessibility, assignment of staff within an agency . . . and reimbursement for services, have been shown to be stronger determinants of underservice than attitudes.
>
> (Gatz and Pearson, 1988)

Respondents to Murphy's survey also felt that organizational factors, such as separation of older persons' services into separate healthcare trusts, and contractual issues were important. There seemed an awareness of the unmet need by the service providers, but insufficient resources to encourage expansion of psychotherapy services into the older age range.

A survey by Collins *et al.* (1997) looked at the attitudes of general medical practitioners (GPs) in the UK to referral of older people with depression for psychological treatments. Despite positive intentions little referral activity was forthcoming. Ninety-three per cent of GPs would consider referring an older person for psychological help but only 44 per cent had actually done so. The GPs showed lack of knowledge of the range of interventions available and the indications for choosing a particular psychological therapy. The authors suggest that more education and training, especially for GPs with little psychiatry experience, would be likely to contribute to more effective use of services.

So it seems that while professionals accept the need to expand psychological therapy services to meet the need in the older population, a range of organizational and historical factors have prevented this from happening. It is unlikely that significant amounts of resources are going to be diverted from more acute areas of service provision within medicine as a whole, so it must be the responsibility of those who already work with older people to make a start, and not before time. Initially, this process will be aided by an understanding of the effectiveness of available therapies.

Evaluation of psychological therapies

All clinicians practising psychological therapies will, in some way, be engaged in evaluation of the treatments they deliver. At the very least they will use simple steps to measure their patients' response to treatment, such as progress on therapy goals or outcome on symptom rating scales. Then, if an intervention has been successful with one patient, the clinician will be curious to know whether other patients might benefit, such as others with the same disorder or those of a similar age. As well as clinicians, other groups, such as potential patients and commissioners of psychological therapy services, will also have an interest in the effectiveness and generalisability of a therapy. There is, therefore, a need to have access to any evidence of a therapy's benefits in clinical trials (efficacy) or everyday practice (effectiveness).

The simplest form of evidence that is published is usually the case report, in which new therapeutic strategies or applications are described and demonstrated. Beyond this, the next most sophisticated level of evidence will be a series of cases in which a standardized therapeutic approach has been applied to a range of patients with similar problems. After this, the most rigorous level of investigation involves standardization of the therapy and applying it systematically to a large group of patients with very similar characteristics, usually in a randomized controlled trial (RCT). Once a therapy has been evaluated in this way and its efficacy demonstrated, its use may then be broadened in the further development of therapeutic interventions (Salkovskis 1995).

In looking at the evidence for the efficacy of a particular therapy, the clinician or commissioner will be particularly interested in any RCTs that exist. It is important, however, to consider how applicable a trial is to the therapist's own patients. The therapist needs to consider questions such as patient characteristics (e.g. age, gender, whether hospitalized or living at home) and choice of outcome measures (e.g. reduction in score on rating scales, no longer achieving case level on diagnostic criteria, improvement in functioning, use of healthcare services). The age of patients in trials is of course very important for clinicians treating older adults. Treatments which are efficacious with younger adults cannot be automatically assumed to have the same results with older adults. Trials that do include older adults may favour patients who are easy to recruit (such as through media advertisements) and exclude those encountered in routine practice – for example, those with concurrent severe physical illness. Additional questions for the clinician are whether the treatment described is feasible in the setting proposed, whether it could harm the patients and whether the therapy will be influenced by the patient's values (Straus and McAlister 2001).

Of the therapies described in this book the largest evidence base exists for cognitive behaviour therapy (CBT) and interpersonal therapy (IPT). The efficacy of IPT as an acute treatment and a maintenance treatment for major depression in younger adults has been well demonstrated (DiMascio *et al.* 1974, Weissman *et al.* 1974, 1979, 1981, Elkin *et al.* 1989, Frank *et al.* 1990, 1991). The benefits of IPT with older adults have also been demonstrated in the Maintenance Therapies in Late-Life Depression study (MTLLD) (Reynolds *et al.* 1999) which examined the effects of IPT and the antidepressant nortriptyline, alone and in combination, as maintenance treatments in depression. Patients were 60 and over with current major depression and a previous history of depression. Those whose depression remitted with a combination of IPT and antidepressant were randomized to receive one of four maintenance treatments (IPT and antidepressant; IPT and placebo; medication clinic and antidepressant; or medication clinic and placebo) over three years of monthly follow-up. The combination of antidepressant and IPT was the most powerful in preventing a recurrence of major depression in 80 per cent of subjects; and in older subjects (70 and older) rates of recurrence were higher and more rapid except in the combination treatment group. In the younger patients, all three active treatments were equally effective in preventing relapse. Given that relapse of depressive illness is such a major problem for elderly patients, this study is a reminder of the potential importance of psychological treatment in the maintenance treatment of depression. For a more detailed account of clinical and outcome correlates in the MTLLD, see Wolfson *et al.* (1997) and Reynolds, *et al.* (1999).

The efficacy of CBT as an acute phase treatment for depressive illness has also been clearly demonstrated in a number of controlled trials with adults of working age (Williams 1997). There is increasing evidence to support its role as a maintenance treatment. Paykel *et al.* (1999) demonstrated that in patients with residual depressive symptoms who continued to receive pharmacotherapy, cognitive therapy reduced relapse rates one year after treatment with a relative risk reduction of 38 per cent. On the whole, the efficacy of CBT as a treatment for depression in older adults can only be inferred from work with younger adults. In support of this, a meta-analysis of forty-eight trials with adults of all ages found no association between effect size and age (Gloaguen *et al.* 1998). The few trials with older adults that have been published are of small size, but demonstrate a positive effect size compared with waiting list controls and psychodynamic and behaviour therapies (Koder *et al.* 1996). A small study comparing CBT with lithium maintenance (Wilson *et al.* 1995) demonstrated improved outcome at one year in the CBT group. CBT can also have significant benefit in a specific group of older adults, dementia carers (Marriott *et al.* 2000).

Of the other therapies described in this book there has been relatively little evaluation with older adults. In part this probably reflects the difficulty in evaluating outcomes which are not based on symptom severity or diagnostic criteria, and are harder to measure, such as the mobilization of a family's resources or modification of long-standing characterological traits. Evaluation of systemic therapy with the elderly includes a family intervention to alleviate carer burden in dementia (Mittelman *et al.* 1993). Cognitive analytic therapy has not been evaluated with older adults, and with younger adults research is at the level of case series (Ryle and Golynkina 2000). Early outcome data from the Guy's Borderline Project, however, is providing support for the view that CAT is likely to be an effective intervention for people with borderline personality disorder. Therefore, there remains a need for ongoing evaluation of the full range of therapies, as well as a need to replicate existing research with larger patient samples (Almeida 2000).

Despite the importance of remaining informed of current research, the clinician may have some difficulty in accessing and appraising the full range of evidence. For this reason, systematic reviews are increasingly being performed. These quantitative summaries apply 'scientific strategies that limit bias to the . . . assembly, critical appraisal and synthesis of all relevant studies on a specific topic' (Cook *et al.* 1995). The Cochrane Collaboration database of systematic reviews (www.cohrane.org) is a useful source and already includes reviews of some psychological interventions in dementia (but not including the therapies described in this book).

Another benefit of systematic reviews is that they can highlight unanswered research questions. These might include whether psychotherapies with older adults could improve relapse rates of depression, or whether interventions in institutions and with cognitively impaired patients are effective. Answers to these questions will help us to decide the best role of psychotherapies in the armoury of treatments available and their place in the services we plan for the future. There is a need for evaluation of psychotherapeutic services themselves through large sample surveys of psychotherapy recipients and research on the psychotherapeutic process. Such practice-based research will complement the evidence base of clinical trials, and practice research networks would help to pool data relating to clinical outcomes to obtain high-quality clinical databases on large clinically representative samples to measure effectiveness of services (Parry 2000). The process of psychotherapy research and its relationship to service evaluation and improvements in patient care are usefully summarized by Roth *et al.* (1996).

Making the choice of therapy

Within this book we have considered factors that make an individual patient broadly suitable for a particular therapy. We have considered efficacy and principles around the best use of the existing evidence base. Illustrations will have served to some extent to illuminate the application of methods of treatment to individual patients. We will now consider possible goals of therapy and the factors involved in the choice of treatment for an individual patient. See box 7.1.

Consider Mr Patrick aged 85 years:

> Mr Patrick became increasingly nervous on growing older and, following a mild stroke, he moved temporarily to his son's house. He was clinically depressed when seen and feeling disappointed with life with the family. He felt excluded and increasingly voiced the view that he was only wanted financially and would prefer to move back home. In his new neighbourhood he was now cut off from contacts with friends and former pleasurable pastimes. He believed his son now saw him as incapable of managing alone, and also complained that his son was too busy to be involved in discussion of the treatment plan.

For Mr Patrick there is a range of potentially helpful psychological interventions. These could be considered alone or in conjunction with physical and social interventions – for example, psychotropic medication and support to develop new social and recreational activities. Psychological treatments with best evidence of efficacy in depression are IPT and CBT, but there is also evidence of effectiveness of psychodynamic work and family therapy. IPT could focus on role dispute. Since the loss of his old roles, the new balance of power may constitute a problem area with a link to the depression. Therapy might provide the structure for Mr Patrick to explore and come to a realistic evaluation of exactly what he has lost. Mr Patrick could work to identify his own needs and take more responsibility for choosing how to meet these. He could try other strategies for negotiation with his son. CBT could help him to understand and manage his depressive symptoms and adopt a problem-solving approach to his difficulties. Family therapy might initially seem impossible given that Mr Patrick's son is so busy. However, his son might be pleased to have the opportunity to share his feelings about how hard he is trying, to no apparent avail. A psychodynamic intervention might focus on the sources of low self-esteem and fear of abandonment stemming from early life experience. CAT might identify the core reciprocal roles being enacted between father and son – for example, Rejecting to Rejected, Critical to Helpless and Striving with Covert Anger.

A recommendation on the type of therapy will be shaped by evidence on efficacy balanced with the applicability in any particular context. As we have seen in this chapter, during the earlier stages of evaluation of a therapy relatively pure conditions are usually studied to establish efficacy. While the presence of a medical condition or sensory impairment may influence the efficacy, just such factors act as triggers to psychological problems. Later life is a period of active change in a person's social and biological context, and a

---

Box 7.1 Choice of psychological therapy

Recommendation of a therapy is based on:
- Treatment efficacy
- Likelihood of effectiveness in this current situation
- Potential for an appropriate rapport with the therapist
- Severity and time scale of problem and timing of intervention
- Availability of required level of experience and/or supervision
- Patient preference
- Motivation
- Cultural and ethnic considerations

number of contributory or aetiological factors may be present. The presence of a serious medical condition might be seen as a contra-indication for IPT because it might disrupt attendance at therapy sessions. However, the therapy may clinically make sense as a treatment for depression, with the role transition as a focus for therapy.

Consideration may be given to meeting individual needs in the presence of impairment in sensory, language, memory or writing skills. The use of therapy manuals, information sheets, taping of sessions, and letters or phone calls to remind about tasks or to provide feedback from sessions can be considered. Until there is more research into efficacy in the presence of co-morbidity, a trade-off between practical adaptation and possible lowering of efficacy will remain an issue both at the individual treatment level and service provision level.

For all psychotherapies there is a requirement for the develop-ment of an appropriate therapist–patient relationship. The thera-peutic models pose different demands on making and sustaining rapport. In IPT the therapist adopts an advocate position, taking an active role (indeed even a 'role model'), and may participate in role-play to support the patient in trying out new styles of interacting. CBT requires exchange with the therapist such as to form an alliance that facilitates learning from the therapist in order to dis-tinguish thoughts, feelings and behaviour. In CAT the therapist adopts a non-expert but collaborative relationship in order to jointly develop a shared view of past life influences and unconscious material. There is less central emphasis on the current relationship with the therapist than in psychodynamic therapy where the therap-ist will work through the transference relationship. This relation-ship will require of the patient the capacity to self-explore. Ability in the patient to tolerate frustration within the therapy and the rela-tionship will be needed. In family therapy, generally the therapist will work from a position of neutrality, attempting to respect mem-bers from different generations as equals, and credit the different positions and problems of the family's constituent members.

Consider Mr Richards:

> Mr Richards has been experiencing recurring episodes of depression for five years despite taking a mood stabilizer which he does not wish to change. The pattern has been of illnesses lasting several months, responding well once he reaches the

point of agreeing to a review of his medication. However, it is not without considerable concern to his family that there is usually a period of very poor quality of life until this point is reached on each occasion. He is seen in the recovery phase.

His difficulties could be addressed in a number of ways using psychological treatment skills. He might be helped to address his unwillingness to change his prophylactic medication. A psychological intervention might also augment his current medication regime or be used after recovery to reduce risk of relapse.

The options for psychological treatment will be influenced by the acuteness of the present situation. If there is a crisis such as with breakdown of care, poor hydration and subsequent dehydration and delirium, then options are limited. Preliminary psychological intervention may include family meetings (with or without the patient), whereas a CBT or IPT intervention may be precluded. The severity of a current depressive illness may limit therapy choice. Mr Richards may or may not have sufficient concentration and motivation to be able to work with the therapist. Presence of psychotic symptoms in Mr Richards's illness would preclude early use of psychological treatment, but in such severe illness psychological treatment may be used in combination with medication. Once the crisis has passed, but while Mr Richards remains symptomatic, then options particularly to consider include CBT and IPT. He might benefit from learning strategies for future prevention as offered within these treatment models. Psychodynamic or family interventions may also be considered for symptom improvement. After recovery, they may play a role in addressing factors surrounding risk of further episodes. Had he previously tried CBT but been unable to progress, or problematic and enduring personality traits had co-existed, then he might be a candidate for CAT.

Recommendation of a therapy should also be based on awareness of the quality of treatment that is accessible to the patient. Knowledge of the availability of an appropriate level of therapist experience and supervision to match the complexity of the patient's difficulties is an issue at the point of advising on options.

Patient preferences will be important, but advice should specify treatment for which there is clear evidence of efficacy for the condition presented. In order to develop preference the patient needs to know what is on offer and what the treatment will involve. He or she will also need to have an idea of the scope and extent of possible change for the better. Patients also need to have sufficient information about the nature, format and length of the treatment options in order to judge whether a therapy offered has the potential to be a helpful exercise for them. Therapeutic techniques and language of therapy may be alien and need explanation. For example, the patient would need to know that in CBT she might expect to learn certain skills to help with problems and to have the opportunity to try these out, and that the focus of the therapy is on the here-and-now rather than exploring earlier life stages.

The predominant techniques need to be ones that are acceptable. In IPT this will include communication analysis and practice of learned skills outside of sessions. In CBT there is a requirement to learn how to record current conscious thoughts. By contrast, in psychodynamic therapy the therapist's active listening will result in the patient being in receipt of the therapist's interpretation and own associations. In CAT there are activities such as diary-keeping, rating and recording, prose writing, and construction of diagrams. In family therapy, meeting together with other key people is facilitated. The therapeutic tools also include dialogue and undertaking some recommended activities outside of sessions.

An appropriate level of motivation is needed for all therapies. This has been detailed in the chapters. The patient needs some degree of willingness to start to think about themselves or their problems in psychological terms, and to have some understanding compatible with the theoretical model. The precise requirements of motivation vary. For example, since IPT places the locus of responsibility within a disease framework, motivation is needed to explore current relationship issues from a sick-role position. Symptoms are 'caused' by the depression, which will go away. CBT, however, will necessitate motivation to recognize and explore distorted thoughts and link these with feelings. In individual CAT, patients will need to be motivated to work with the therapist to construct an understanding of the part played by unconscious factors from the past. Reformulation of a life story with the therapist can help the person engage and develop motivation as they recognize they have been listened to. Family therapy implicitly requires the interest and motivation of those other than the patient, although participants do not need to share the therapist's theoretical perspective of the problem resting within the family rather than the individual. Psychodynamic therapy requires a greater degree of responsibility for the presence of symptoms, and motivation to explore this and take on board and 'digest' interpretation.

Where the patient's cultural background is not the same as that of the therapist there is a need on the part of the therapist for sensitivity to potential economic, language and discriminatory barriers. These may be cultural differences through race, gender and religion, or subcultural differences such as poverty and poor education. The therapist therefore needs to develop an understanding of the potential impact of culturally determined influences within the therapy and therapeutic relationship for each individual. Cultural differences might influence whether the patient even considers the option of psychological treatments. Fear of value conflicts may deter patients from group treatment if they consider themselves to be at risk from poorly managed conflict with members of the group with different cultural beliefs and values. Therapists need to be as careful not to develop stereotyped views of other cultures as much as they need to be aware of assumptions inherent in their own culture and training background which hamper an appropriate positive experience of therapy for the patient. It is important not to assume cultural stereotypes of family, especially if working from a structural family framework. Age-related cultural issues include the impact of changing values within and between the generations. The type of role disputes that might emerge between generations may be unfamiliar to the therapist, and understanding would be needed.

Cultural influences are reflected in the low levels of availability of trained therapists and access to supervision for work with older people. Psychological treatment services restricting their work to people under the age of 65 do not match the evidence base of efficacy. This may be an indicator of cultural attitudes to older people as well as the wider economics of the care system for older people.

In summary, recommendations on treatment and methods likely to be effective in particular circumstances can be made; and where there is research evidence of efficacy of one particular modality, the patient should be advised of this. Clear information on the scope and techniques used in the possible options can help patients move towards a therapy of choice.

Delivering a service

A model of service provision that is flexible enough to adapt itself to the idiosyncrasies of modern health services is that of the psychological therapies network (PTN). In this structure, professionals who are already doing the hands-on work, and undoubtedly already providing some psychological therapies, are linked, coordinated, supervised, and encouraged to develop their skills and the time they spend engaging in psychological therapies with older people. Core staff thus form a network rather than a department, and the model emphasizes the need to integrate psychological approaches into grass-root service provision rather than creating another 'specialist' service that may seem elitist or have intimidating boundaries that deter access. Such a model has been developing in the county of Somerset in England, and a number of points have emerged as key issues in the successful evolution of the PTN (see Box 7.2).

The points made in Box 7.2 are by no means comprehensive but simply identify actions and areas for consideration that have emerged over a two-year period in Somerset. Each organization will have its unique history, strengths and weaknesses. There is no inherent conflict between a psychotherapy department and a PTN, and both can exist within the same organization. The concept of the network is simply a way of building a service, with the practitioner as the basic structural unit rather than focusing on buildings or a few senior professionals and their particular interests. It is clearly important to have some structures in place before addressing the other major issue behind the lack of psychological therapies provision for older people: the paucity of referrals. If demand and expectations are stimulated before professionals have the time, supervision and support to deliver psychological therapies, then referrers will lose interest or become critical of the service before it is hatched.

The first stage is to generate awareness amongst referrers of the value of psychological therapies in relation to older people, and to challenge any lingering ageist views. Next, it is important to develop some threshold criteria for entry to the service, which are based on severity or need. Referrers can then be educated so that they are able to assess the client with reference to the entry criteria with the result that, on the whole, appropriate clients are referred on. This is perhaps the most difficult task. Many potential referrers will be delighted to hear of a new advance in treatment or opportunity to benefit clients which they had not previously considered, but may then refer with such enthusiasm that the service is overrun with assessment requests and growing waiting lists for actual provision

Box 7.2   How to establish a psychological therapies network (PTN) for older people

- Form an executive committee of senior practitioners and managers for the organization as a whole in order to oversee the evolution of the PTN (psychological therapies network) and to interface with commissioners, funding organizations, users and carers and the wider health services
- Remove all age criteria in operational policies relating to psychological treatments
- Encourage professionals to link across the boundaries of services that use age as a cut-off, and to find their shared interest in a particular psychological therapy
- Survey to identify who is currently doing what therapy, what training they have had and what supervision structures exist
- Identify the psychotherapy modalities that the organization wishes to provide, based on the available evidence and local experience, and define the amount of each that should be available in each locality in terms of practitioner hours per week
- Identify practitioners and practitioner-supervisors in each modality paying heed to the requisites of the relevant umbrella organizations
- Allocate protected time to each practitioner to engage in psychological therapy work
- Appoint a co-ordinator for each locality to act as a trouble shooter and manager of the supervision structures
- Make arrangements for the co-ordinator to meet each practitioner at regular intervals to discuss their role in the PTN and their training needs
- Ensure that those working with older people have equal access to training and supervision compared with those working with younger clients
- Develop rationales for allocating a particular client to a particular therapy
- Collect information on different therapy modalities to enable clients to express informed preferences
- Identify more experienced practitioners who can provide psychotherapy assessments in difficult cases and also act as consultants in the application of psychotherapy principles in grass root clinical work
- Decide under what circumstances the person delivering the psychological therapy can also be the client's care co-ordinator, responsible medical officer or equivalent
- Establish a regular programme of education, training and sharing of ideas and experience
- Establish systems for auditing practice, outcomes and clients' views

of therapies. In the early stages it may be advantageous to target particular referrer groups to generate referrals of a particular client profile. This will allow the service to evolve in a way that is led by need, effectiveness of treatments and local availability rather than the more random and subjective factors that can account for the patchy and inconsistent way in which psychological therapies for older people are currently distributed. For example, following the evidence base, members of the network may target in-patient assessment units to encourage referral of older people with moderate degrees of depression who are likely to be able to engage in CBT as an adjunctive treatment. Alternatively, an experienced psychodynamic practitioner may link to a community mental health team for, say, one hour a week to discuss difficult 'personality disorder' cases and support staff in dealing with their transference and countertransference issues.

It is encouraging that attitudes appear to have warmed to the use of psychological therapies with older people; professionals are generally optimistic about the value of such treatment and referrers are willing to change their practice. It is primarily structural factors that appear to be holding back further development. Planners, managers and providers must consider ways of organizing their services to facilitate the development of psychological therapies for older people, and ways of supporting and encouraging their staff to develop the time, expertise and interest in this valuable work.

References

Almeida, O.P. (2000) Commentary on review of Reynolds *et al.* (1999), *Evidence-based Mental Health* 2: 85.

Collins, E., Katona, C. and Orrell, M.W. (1997) 'Management of depression in the elderly by general practitioners: referral for psychological treatments', *British Journal of Clinical Psychology* 36: 445–448.

Cook, D.J., Sakett, W.O. and Spitzer, W.O. (1995) 'Methodological guidelines for systematic reviews of randomized control trials in health care from the Potsdam Consultation on Meta-Analyis', *Journal of Clinical Epidemiology* 48: 167–171.

DiMascio, A., Weissman, M.M. *et al.* (1974) 'Differential symptom reduction by drugs and psychotherapy in acute depression', *Archives of General Psychiatry* 36: 1450–1456.

Elkin, I., Shea, M.T., Watkins, J.T., *et al.* (1989) 'National Institute of Mental Health treatment of depression collaborative research program:

general effectiveness of treatments', *Archives of General Psychiatry* 46: 971–982.

Frank, E., Kupfer, D.J., Perel, J.M., *et al.* (1990) 'Three-year outcomes for maintenance therapies in recurrent depression', *Archives of General Psychiatry* 47: 1093–1099.

Frank, E., Kupfer, D.J., Wagner, E.F. *et al.* (1991) 'Efficacy of interpersonal psychotherapy as a maintenance treatment of recurrent depression', *Archives of General Psychiatry*, 48: 1053–1059.

Freud, S. (1905) *On Psychotherapy. Standard edition, vol. 7*, London: Hogarth Press.

Gatz, M. and Pearson, C.G. (1988) 'Ageism revised and the provision of psychological services', *American Psychologist* 43: 184–188.

Gloaguen, V., Cottraux, J., Cucherat, M. and Blackburn, I. (1998) 'A meta-analysis of the effects of cognitive therapy in depressed patients', *Journal of Affective Disorders* 49: 59–72.

Koder, D., Brodaty, H. and Anstey, K. (1996) 'Cognitive therapy for depression in the elderly', *International Journal of Geriatric Psychiatry* 11: 98–107.

Marriott, A., Donaldson, C., Tarrier, N. and Burns, A. (2000) 'Effectiveness of cognitive-behavioural therapy family intervention in reducing the burden of care in carers of patients with Alzheimer's disease', *British Journal of Psychiatry* 176: 557–562.

Mittelman, M.S., Ferris, S.H., Steinberg, G. *et al.* (1993) 'An intervention that delays institutionalization of Alzheimer's disease patients: treatment of spouse-caregivers', *Gerontologist* 33: 730–740.

Murphy, S. (2000) 'Provision of psychotherapy services for older people', *Psychiatric Bulletin* 24: 184–187.

Parry, G. (2000) 'Evidence based psychotherapy: special case or special pleading?', *Evidence-based Mental Health* 3: 35–37.

Paykel, E.S., Scott, J., Teasdale, J.D., Johnson, A.L., Garland, A., Moore, R., Jenaway, A., Cornwall, P.L., Hayhurst, H., Abbott, R. and Pope, M. (1999) 'Prevention of relapse in residual depression by cognitive therapy', *Archives of General Psychiatry* 56: 829–835.

Reynolds, C.F., Frank, E., Perel, J.M. *et al.* (1999) 'Nortriptyline and inter-personal psychotherapy as maintenance therapies for recurrent major depression: a randomized controlled trial in patients older than 59 years', *Journal of the American Medical Association* 281(1): 39–45.

Roth, A., Fonagy, P. and Parry, G. (1996) 'Psychotherapy research, funding, and evidence-based practice', in A. Roth and P. Fonagy (eds) *What Works for Whom?* New York: Guilford Press.

Ryle, A. and Golynkina, K. (2000) 'Effectiveness of time-limited cognitive analytic therapy of borderline personality disorder: factors associated with outcome', *British Journal of Medical Psychology* 73: 197–210.

Salkovskis, P.M. (1995) 'Demonstrating specific effects in cognitive and behavioural therapy', in M. Aveline and D. Shapiro (eds) *Research Foundations for Psychotherapy Practice*, Chichester: Wiley.

Straus, S.E. and McAlister, F. (2001) 'Applying the results of trials and systematic reviews to our individual patients', *Evidence-based Mental Health* 4: 6–7.

Weissman, M.M., Klerman, G.L., Paykel, E.S. *et al.* (1974) 'Treatment effects on the social adjustment of depressed patients', *Archives of General Psychiatry* 30: 771–778.

Weissman, M.M., Prusott, B.A., DiMascio, A. *et al.* (1979) 'The efficacy of drugs and psychotherapy in the treatment of acute depressive episodes', *American Journal of Psychiatry* 136: 555–558.

Weissman, M.M., Klerman, G.L., Prusoff, B.A. *et al.* (1981) 'Depressed outpatients: results one year after treatment with drugs and/or interpersonal psychotherapy', *Archives of General Psychiatry* 38: 52–55.

Williams, J.M.G. (1997) 'Depression', in D.M. Clark and C.G. Fairburn (eds) *Science and Practice of Cognitive Behaviour Therapy*, Oxford: Oxford University Press.

Wilson, K.C.M., Scott, M., Abou-Saleh, M., Burns, R. and Copeland, J.R.M. (1995) 'Long-term effects of cognitive-behavioural therapy and lithium therapy on depression in the elderly', *British Journal of Psychiatry* 167: 653–658.

Wolfson, L., Miller, M.D., Houck, P. *et al.* (1997) 'Foci interpersonal psychotherapy (IPT) in depressed elders: clinical and outcome correlates in a combined IPT/Nortriptyline Protocol', *Psychotherapy Research* 7(1): 45–55.

Index